101 Inspirational Stories

from the World's

Best Flute Players

Edited by John D. Sinclair

Windplayer Publications

Library of Congress Cataloging-in-Publication Data

Flute stories : 101 inspirational stories from the world's best flute players / edited by John Sinclair.— 1st ed.

   p. cm.

Includes index.

  ISBN 1-930237-10-3 (pbk.)

1. Flute players—Biography. I. Sinclair, John D., 1971-

  ML399.F57 2003

   788.3'2'0922—dc22

                                   2003016551

Copyright © 2003 Windplayer Publications

Windplayer Publications

PO Box 2750, Malibu CA 90265

(800) 946-3305

www.windplayer.com

All rights reserved. No part of this book shall be reproduced, stored in a retrieval system, or transmitted by any means – electronic, mechanical, photocopying, recording, or otherwise – without written permission from the publisher, except for the inclusion of brief quotations in a review.

ISBN 1-930237-10-3

Printed in the United States of America

First Edition: August 2003

cover design and layout: Todd Allen Design

"The highest purpose of art is to inspire."

– Bob Dylan

preface

Over the past few days I have become engrossed in reading an advance copy of "Flute Stories: 101 Inspirational Stories from the World's Best Flute Players." The list of contributors reads like an international who's who of flute playing. The stories told by these legendary flute players are truly inspirational and eye-opening. It is comforting, uplifting, and informative to see that even the most successful musicians of our time have faced many of the same difficulties and hurdles that we all face.

The contributing players in this unique book have achieved success in every style of music-making, from classical to rock to jazz, and they come from every corner of the globe. The stories they have to share make for riveting reading from cover to cover.

My congratulations to Windplayer Publications for doing such a splendid job in creating this unique publication, and to every contributor for sharing their important and often deeply personal stories with everyone.

—Larry Krantz, *www.larrykrantz.com*

foreword)))

Who knew that the path to success as a world-class flute player could involve working at Pizza Hut or picking strawberries? Or having to teach yourself bass violin just to get a spot in an orchestra? Or being told by your musical idol that you don't stand a chance as a professional flutist and should start looking for another line of work?

These are the stories from the people at the top — the flutists who met the challenges, struggled through the tough times, and ultimately made it in the competitive world of professional musicianship. Without exception, every flute player in this book has a place somewhere among the world's most talented, brilliant, respected, and successful musicians.

That is not to say that this collection is exhaustive, and there are various reasons why some outstanding flute players could not be included. Some were impossibly busy, on the move, or otherwise difficult to contact, and a few politely declined to be interviewed. If someone's name isn't here, that doesn't mean it shouldn't be.

But of the 101 world-renowned flutists who *do* appear in this book, each gave generously of their time, insight, and experiences, and the results are priceless. Their backgrounds cover the spectrum from Alabama to Zurich, from thronging Beijing and cosmopolitan New York to the tiny mountain villages of Venezuela. There are flutists who fought in World War II and others who were still in school when the Berlin Wall took a tumble. There are legends like Julius Baker, celebrated for a lifetime of accomplishment, and young artists such as Catherine Ransom and Davide Formisano who have just begun blazing trails. There are those, like Jeanne Baxtresser, who have earned top chairs in the world's most distinguished orchestras, and others, such as Robert Dick, who risked everything to find fulfillment on the independent pathway. There are pioneers like Frances Blaisdell, the first female flutist for the New York Philharmonic, and Herbie Mann, who was playing jazz back when no one thought the flute could be a jazz instrument. There are revered conservatory teachers like Robert Willoughby and popular artists, like Ian Anderson, who were schooled on stage.

Their stories range from lighthearted to deeply emotional, from the many struggles of studenthood to the serious issues that a musician can face at any point in his or her career. Here you'll find great and horrible

Foreword

teachers, failed auditions and sudden windfalls, overwhelmed parents straining to balance kids and career, crooked embouchures and agonizing technical problems, minimum-wage jobs and career breakthroughs, battles with life-threatening illness, the patient triumph of nursing an injury back to health, and the sheer joy of living a life devoted to music.

Every single one of these stories is unique, but all 101 flutists have one thing in common — they never gave up. If you play the flute — or if you aspire to any artistic calling — you'll find stories here that speak to your own questions, frustrations, goals, and experiences, regardless of the path you're following.

—John Sinclair, Editor

table of contents)))

Ian Anderson	1
Yossi Arnheim	4
Lars Asbjørnsen	6
Don Bailey	8
Julius Baker	10
Clement Barone	12
Jeanne Baxtresser	14
Janne Bengtson	17
William Bennett	20
Jacob Berg	23
Jean Berkenstock	25
Emily Beynon	27
Frances Blaisdell	29
Wissam Boustany	32
Randolph Bowman	34
Bonita Boyd	37
Margaret Campbell	39
Catherine Cantin	42
Celia Chambers	44
Kathleen Chastain	46
Ann Cherry	48
Sandra Church	50
Tadeu Coelho	52
Robert Cole	55
David Cramer	58
Gareth Davies	60
Philippa Davies	63
Timothy Day	65
Michel Debost	68
Robert Dick	70
Louise Di Tullio	73
Aralee Dorough	75
Elena Durán	78
Moshe Aron Epstein	81

Flute Stories

Andy Findon	84
Davide Formisano	86
Patrick Gallois	88
James Galway	91
Bradley Garner	93
Laura Gilbert	95
Scott Goff	97
Bernard Goldberg	99
Erich Graf	101
Peter-Lukas Graf	103
Matej Grahek	106
Marco Granados	108
Marc Grauwels	111
Susan Greenberg	113
Susan Hoeppner	116
Trudy Kane	118
Mindy Kaufman	120
Katherine Kemler	122
Jeffrey Khaner	124
Stephen Kujala	126
Walfrid Kujala	129
Robert Langevin	131
Rhonda Larson	133
Hubert Laws	135
Herbie Mann	137
Göran Marcusson	139
Robin McKee	142
Susan Milan	143
Matt Molloy	146
Ervin Monroe	149
Claude Monteux	152
Alexander Murray	154
Emmanuel Pahud	156
Susan Palma-Nidel	159

Table of Contents

Michael Parloff	161
Donald Peck	164
James Pellerite	166
Catherine Ransom	168
Alison Young Rasch	171
Paul Renzi	174
Paula Robison	177
Elizabeth Rowe	179
Gary Schocker	181
David Shostac	183
Nora Shulman	186
Renée Siebert	188
Emily Skala	190
Christina Smith	193
Joshua Smith	195
Jonathan Snowden	197
Clare Southworth	199
Mark Sparks	201
Alexa Still	204
Sheridon Stokes	206
Mary Stolper	208
Jin Ta	211
Dave Valentin	214
Jim Walker	216
Brooks de Wetter-Smith	218
Robert Willoughby	221
Ransom Wilson	223
Carol Wincenc	226
John Wion	228
Trevor Wye	230
Anne Diener Zentner	232
Matthias Ziegler	234
Laurel Zucker	236
Eugenia Zukerman	238

Flute Stories

Ian Anderson

Ian Anderson)))

Ian Anderson is known throughout the world of rock music as the flute and voice behind the legendary Jethro Tull. Still enjoying its lengthy career, including ongoing performances worldwide, Jethro Tull has released 30 albums and sold more than 60 million copies. In addition, Anderson performs his solo work with orchestras, and his fourth solo album will be available in fall of 2003. For more information, check out www.j-tull.com.

I started off learning to play the guitar, and I played it until the age of 19, when I heard Eric Clapton for the first time. I became aware that I was never going to be that good and that I should look around for something else to play that wouldn't stand me in endless comparison with the guy who was — and in many ways still is — the number one guitar player of the millennium.

So I decided to trade in my trusty Fender Stratocaster — probably worth about $15,000 today — for anything that caught my eye in the music store. What caught my eye was my very first Shure microphone.

And hanging on the wall above it, a flute.

It was a spontaneous, spur-of-the-moment thing. I had no awareness of flute playing, and I took this thing out of the shop without the faintest idea of how to play it. Of course, flutes don't come with instruction manuals, and after three or four months, I gave up on the idea. I tried, but couldn't make anything useful out of it musically, so I just left it in its box.

I began playing tin whistle and harmonica in a band which had formed during my years in art school. We got a new guitar player, Mick Abrahams, and that was the beginning of Jethro Tull. I went back and finally began to get a few notes out of the flute, and as Jethro Tull began its very first shows, I began learning how to play the flute onstage.

Jeffrey Hammond, who later joined Jethro Tull as a bass player, had just acquired an album by Roland Kirk, which he played for me. That kind of put the seal on it for me — here was another flute player who was doing something that wasn't classical music. The first fully-fledged flute instrumental I learned to play was in fact a Roland Kirk piece called "Serenade to a Cuckoo."

I've always been quite flattered by the fact that there is some attention paid to me in serious musical circles. I am at least noted (not necessarily lauded or approved of) as being one of those people who has brought the flute into a different area of music and carved out a niche. To be recognized is very flattering. I don't think any traditionally academic flute players would say, "Ian Anderson is a great flute player." They might say, "He's kind of an interesting flute player because of what he does, in the musical context in which he does it."

I've never set out to be a technically good player. Because I didn't have any lessons, I didn't know how to evoke the purity of tone that classical players are able to get. I deliberately went for a rough, edgy sound that would cut through the rock band instrumentation. I improvised and tried to make the flute emulate the kinds of motifs, riffs, and solos that I would have played on guitar. In a way, I turned my flute playing into an imitation of Eric Clapton and Jimi Hendrix. I used the flute in the same musical role as a lead instrument.

I like to use my open-holed concert flute as if it were a bamboo flute or a primitive flute and half-uncover holes to play quarter tones (called bending a note in guitar terms) for emotional effect. And I don't like using the degree of vibrato that is typical in orchestral playing. I do play with vibrato, but I don't use it all the time. In a passage, I will play some notes very straight and literally. It's all a matter of light and shade.

A lot of the time I'm not looking for technical precision. Sometimes playing every note precisely in tune, exactly in tempo, might be okay, but it has an emotional flatness. I'm looking for the nuances — the less-than-perfect performance that has a bit of magic to it.

I have found myself aware from time to time of other flute players in the world of rock music, but none of them have perhaps had the degree of international success that Jethro Tull has. So after all these years, I have the dubious honor of probably being, at the same time, the best and worst flute player in rock 'n' roll.

Flute Stories

Yossi Arnheim)))

Yossi Arnheim is principal flutist with the Israel Philharmonic Orchestra. In addition to his work as with numerous chamber ensembles, his group Sheshbesh, and his East Wind flute and harp duo, he has performed with many orchestras worldwide, including the South-German Chamber Orchestra, the China National Symphony, and the City of London Sinfonia. Arnheim serves on the faculty of the Academy of Music in Jerusalem. For more information, visit www.tau.ac.il/~arnheim.

*W*hen we're classically trained, we learn that whatever's on the page is what we play, and there's not much room for spontaneity. Often we just don't take risks. But a few years ago I learned that I could lift my performance into a whole new dimension, by being a little open-minded about this point.

It started when I decided to do something different from the usual classical music that I've always played. Since I have a family background in Arabic culture, I formed a group to perform Middle Eastern music called Sheshbesh, which began as a trio, including an oud player and a percussionist. However, Middle Eastern music is largely about improvisation, which is something I had never touched before, so we made arrangements of the pieces with my flute parts written out.

We were invited to play a festival in Germany that involved contemporary music. During the intermission of our concert the festival manager introduced us to another musician. He said, "This guy is a percussionist and would love to play something with you." We thought, what could he play with us? We were performing composed pieces that were largely written out, and he couldn't just jump in and wing it. But our percussionist said, "Don't worry about it. Let him come up for the encore. We'll play something with him — we don't know yet what, but we'll play something."

At the end of the concert, the guest came onstage and our percussionist started a 4/4 rhythm. Here I was, standing in front of the microphone, not knowing what was going to happen. Our oud player started to improvise and compose a melody. I began playing long notes and tried to learn the pattern. But by the time I'd nearly learned it, they started playing solos.

If somebody the day before had told me, "Tomorrow you're going to improvise a solo," I would have said, "No." But it just happened that I couldn't refuse. You can't be the flutist in a situation like this and not play solos without looking really stupid. So when it was my turn, I decided, "whatever comes up, comes up." I did some sort of improvisation — I didn't know what, but I felt like I was really flying in heaven. And when I finished, I knew I could do it.

Since then, not only have we brought improvised flute solos into our performances, but I feel much more free in my classical playing as well. That experience made me realize music belongs to the moment. It may be written down or not, but something has to happen when you play it onstage — something that never happened before.

This is the essence of performance — this is what makes it fun. And when we have fun, so does the audience.

Flute Stories

Lars Asbjørnsen)))

As a soloist, Lars Asbjørnsen has performed throughout Europe, Japan, and the United States, including concerto appearances with many prestigious chamber orchestras. He performs at festivals for classical and contemporary music and has had several pieces composed for him. Asbjørnsen is much sought after as a teacher, frequently giving masterclasses at home and abroad. He serves on the faculty of the Wiesbaden Academy of Music in Wiesbaden, Germany. For more information, visit www.norflute.com.

When I was a student at the conservatory, I experienced a situation which helped shape me as a musician and later as a teacher of my own students.

When you're young, self-doubt is very much a part of your budding professional life. I don't know if it's different in the United States than in Europe, but as students we act with a certain cockiness — we're supposed to be self-assured. But a lot of us are full of doubt. "Do I work hard enough? Am I talented enough? What am I going to do? Am I going to be successful?" I know that I asked those questions every day.

I remember watching Isaac Stern on television and he said something along these lines: "You should only become a musician when you are really never in doubt that that's what you have to do." In one way I felt strengthened by his words, but in another way I felt very insecure because I thought, "How can you ever be so sure about it?"

I was somewhere in my mid-20s, approaching the end of my studies at the Folkwanghochschule in Germany, when my professor Matthias Rütters took the time to sit down and have a talk with me. He was a great teacher, and he had a wonderful quality — he never talked badly about a student in the presence of other students. So we felt very safe with him. I trusted him indefinitely, and I had this feeling that he never stopped working with you, preparing you for the future.

That day Rütters sat me down and asked me the simple questions everybody needs to be asked: "What are your ambitions with your music? What are your dreams? What do you think is realistic?" After listening to me for awhile, he said in a very businesslike tone, "Well, I think that can be done. I will help you."

That was very important — that somebody was willing to help shoulder the responsibility for my success. What he was saying, essentially, was that we were both part of a team. He told me, "I will tell you when you're good enough. You just work and don't worry."

Having self-doubt doesn't mean you're worthless. Those kinds of reflections are a healthy and important part of being an artist. But on the other hand, it's important for teachers to be aware of those doubts and to say, "Even if you fail, I will be part of the responsibility for that."

I'm very grateful for that day with my professor — having somebody tell me "it's doable, it's realistic, I will help you." I never succumbed to nerves after that. During dark or difficult moments, it's something I've always been able to think about.

Flute Stories

Don Bailey)))

As a soloist, recitalist and chamber musician, Don Bailey has performed throughout the United States and Europe. He has taught flute at several universities, served on the boards of the Texas, Louisiana, and New York flute clubs, and performed with the Aspen Festival Orchestra, the Dallas Chamber and Bach Orchestras, and the Shreveport Symphony. His debut CD "Voyage," with the Arcata String Quartet, was recently released on the Summit label. For more information, check out http://donbailey.net.

My career is different from most flutists, because I never really wanted to have a career in music. I got into it because I love to play and I'm sort of a natural at it. I went on to get scholarships and then degrees, and one thing led to another, but I've actually left music several times.

It's so difficult having a career in music that if it's not in your gut and in your soul, you shouldn't be doing it. In school we were always told, "You want to be the world's best flute player and get the greatest teaching jobs and the greatest playing jobs." But the idea of making music into a "job" seemed to somehow compartmentalize it and compromise my love of playing.

I initially went to grad school for psychology, but realized I couldn't live without the flute and switched to music instead. Then I got a job teaching music. Everybody wants a teaching job, and I was lucky to get one, but after four years I didn't want it anymore, so I tried to get a degree in hospital administration.

I eventually ended up in New York again, playing flute gigs. I kept running away and coming back. I even went to therapy once, and the therapist made me talk to an empty chair, which was supposed to represent music. The exercise made me realize I was really angry with music, because you work so hard in grad school, and either you can't get good work, or you get a job you don't enjoy or that doesn't pay well. But then listening to a great flute player or instrumentalist always made me want to play again. Or I'd have a great rehearsal or collaboration, and my inspiration would come back. I just knew I should be playing the flute, but I always resisted the idea of locking it into a job.

After many years I found an answer to my problem. It used to be that to have a second career was something flutists were ashamed to admit, because it seemed to say we were failures. The truth of the matter is, I actually do have a second career — I'm an independent contractor/project manager for international law firms. I work four days a week, and the rest of the time I can now afford to make music the way I want to. Financially, I'm in a position to hire good musicians, make recordings, and play concerts.

I've finally come back to where I was at the beginning — doing it just for my own enjoyment. I had to make my own way, and it feels absolutely right.

Flute Stories

Julius Baker)))

Julius Baker has received the National Flute Association Lifetime Achievement Award. During his long and world-renowned career, he has served as principal flute for the Cleveland Orchestra, the Pittsburgh Symphony, the CBS Orchestra, the Chicago Symphony Orchestra, and the New York Philharmonic. He now serves on the faculties of The Juilliard School and The Curtis Institute of Music.

I owe my career to two people: Mitchell Miller and Maurice Sharp.

I was admitted into the Curtis Institute of Music after I graduated from high school in 1933. But before I could attend, Curtis sent me a letter saying they could not accept new students after all, because they did not have enough funding. So Curtis was closed temporarily. I didn't want to waste that year, so I went to the Eastman School of Music instead.

That season I got a letter from Curtis saying they had opened up again for next year, and the flute instructor William Kincaid wanted to hear me play. I had no way of getting there, but my good friend Mitchell Miller had a car and happened to be heading that direction. Mitch had just graduated from Eastman and was heading down to play oboe in the first performance of "Porgy and Bess." He drove me from Rochester to Philadelphia, where I played for Mr. Kincaid. I went on to graduate from Curtis in 1937.

In high school I had studied under Maurice Sharp, who was first flute of the Cleveland Orchestra. He had always encouraged me, and it turned out that just when I was graduating from Curtis, the Cleveland Orchestra had an opening for second flute. Maurice asked me to come in, and that's how I began my career.

I was very lucky. I had two guys, Mitch and Maurice, who were my champions from the very beginning.

Flute Stories

Clement Barone)))

Clement Barone served as piccolo player for the Detroit Symphony Orchestra for 32 years. He authored the book "Learning the Piccolo" (Edutainment). Barone taught for 16 years at the University of Michigan and for 34 years at Wayne State University in Detroit. Previously he played with the Houston Symphony.

*I*n 1975 I had a very serious operation. I had a cancerous saliva gland which had to be taken out, and by doing that, they had to cut the nerves in my throat so that my tongue was crooked.

Before the operation the doctors didn't know that I was a musician. They were going to sever the nerves completely, which meant my tongue would be totally limp. My wife told them I was the piccolo player for the Detroit Symphony Orchestra, and if possible, could they do something to avoid ending my music career? So, this Dr. Stein did the job and left it possible for me to play again. The incision was on the right side of my face, from my ear to the middle of my chin, and down to my chest. To this day it's still numb.

I was at the Ford Hospital in Detroit for four or five weeks. When the doctors had first given me my diagnosis, I thought, "How many years do I have left now to see the sunlight?" But with help and inspiration from my wife, the day after I came out of the operation, I said, "Bring my piccolo."

She brought it, and I went out to the hospital fire escape and tried to blow a note. It was frustrating. Since my tongue was crooked, I couldn't actually tongue for a while. And my embouchure changed because I couldn't feel the pressure of my bottom lip.

I stayed with it. Every day, I'd go to the fire escape and just blow a few notes. I was determined I would play again, and I went back to the orchestra as we were starting the summer season at the fairgrounds. Once I got into that chair, I thought, "No turning back. I have to finish this thing."

I couldn't double-tongue anymore. When you play things like "Scheherazade" or Tchaikovsky's Fourth, and you can't double-tongue, you pray to God your single-tongue can do it. But before I retired in 1991, I played 15 years with no double-tonguing. Many times, when I'd play something with lots of staccato coming up — like Shostakovich's sixth, ninth, or tenth symphonies — I could feel the perspiration run down my back. But I feel that having confidence in your ability is 10 percent of making it through, and the other 90 percent is the guy upstairs.

You put so many hours in to perfect your art. You have to say to yourself, "I've been here this long, I can't give up. I have to work harder now than I've ever worked before." So I relied on faith and determination and praying to God. And every day my wife would help me and tell me it could be done.

I enjoyed my entire career in Detroit. My last 15 years were a trial by error, but I got through it with many complements, and I'm proud that I was able to do it.

Christian Steiner

Jeanne Baxtresser)))

Jeanne Baxtresser has held principal positions with three major orchestras, culminating with her 15-year tenure as solo flutist with the New York Philharmonic. She is recognized internationally as a leading recording artist, author and teacher. She recently released a book with Renée Siebert, "Great Flute Duos From The Orchestral Repertoire" (Theodore Presser) and re-released her debut CD of the Franck Sonata and Schubert Variations. For more information, visit www.jeannebaxtresser.com.

Whenever I've gone through a difficult period in my life, personally or professionally, the flute has always been my salvation. It represents the best and strongest part of me, and it's a refuge from the hard times. You can lose a boyfriend, you can lose money or all kinds of things, but as long as you have that instrument you can go into a room, shut the door and play music.

There were concerts, when I was very young and playing with the Montreal Symphony, where I felt I did the absolute best I could do, and then I'd read one or two reviews afterward that were absolutely crushing.

As musicians we're very vulnerable, because we tend to identify ourselves with how we perform. So if someone says, in effect, "I didn't enjoy how you played," it's an easy jump to thinking, "That person didn't like me, I must not be a good flutist, and therefore I must not be worth very much."

It's hard, but you've got to fight that way of thinking with tremendous energy. I have a system for doing that. When you get a bad review or face some other professional discouragement, you enter a period of what I call mourning. You feel bad, and there's nothing you can do about it except just go through it. A good week is usually what it takes me.

During that time you may not feel like picking the flute up, but it's important to go back in and play fairly soon. Just play a beautiful melody. Feel the instrument and enjoy the tone moving through it. Circumstances can let you down, people can let you down, and sometimes you will not perform up to your own expectations, but don't let those bad feelings interfere with that love you feel for your instrument. Leave the hard times outside the practice room.

After that week of mourning, try to get back and assess what really happened. In the case of a bad review, what made them say those things? Maybe you played well and they didn't know what they were talking about. But can you find a kernel of truth there? Something that will elevate your playing? Consult with friends or play a tape of your performance and try to deal with the situation analytically. Then it's time to say: "I learned, I dealt with it, I'm better for it. Let's go on to the next one, and I know I'll pass through it okay."

I remember analyzing one of those bad reviews very closely. I can't remember what it said, but it made me realize that I had actually played very well, but the problem was that my stance onstage was too rigid. I was like a little wooden soldier, doing my job well but standing there very still. And although I was feeling the music, my lack of motion communicated a sense of stiffness in my playing. I realized I had to loosen up and allow my body to flow more naturally with the music. Because of that review, my barriers broke down and I subsequently grew into a more natural way of playing on stage.

It's important to talk about difficult times with a friend or mentor. One of my greatest relationships was with my teacher, Julius Baker — a great mentor and a friend who helped me do things I never dreamed I could do. I also drew enormous strength from my colleagues, and oddly enough, most of all from the flute players. The people sitting next to you are often considered competitors, but nobody really understands you as well as a fellow flutist does.

My relationship with the flute itself is precious and sacred. Whenever dark times have threatened to pull me down, the flute always seems to be shining up on a hilltop for me, saying, "I'm still here."

Janne Bengtson)))

Janne Bengtson has been solo flutist of the Royal Philharmonic Orchestra since 1989 and for the Royal Opera since 1997, in Stockholm. He is frequently engaged as a soloist, chamber musician, and studio musician in various settings. He has won prizes at international soloist competitions around Europe, and the Swedish composer Johan Hammerth has dedicated a flute concerto to Bengtson. He teaches at the Royal College of Music in Stockholm. For more information, visit www.kanx.se.

Playing the flute has always come naturally to me. I started when I was 4 and achieved success and recognition at an early age, so to stop playing the flute has never been an option, even when critical moments have arisen in my life. In fact, I can think of two specific situations when, due to personal challenges, I reverted and focused on what I think I do best — playing the flute. During those periods, my capabilities as a flute player also developed significantly.

The first situation was at the age of 17. I was about to do my military service in Sweden, and I suddenly faced two different options. One was running out in the fields in rain and storms as a regular soldier for 12 months, which was not very appealing. The other was to apply for the Swedish Army Music Platoon, a very small platoon with the best Swedish musicians born the same year as myself.

The entry barrier was of course huge, so I had to start practicing in a disciplined and focused way, which was the first time in my life I needed to do that. I spent the summer in Greece, and when the hotel guests took their siesta for three to four hours, I was in my room practicing. Strangely, no one complained. I was finally accepted to the Swedish Army as a flute player and had a wonderful year.

The second situation was much more dramatic and happened when I was 24. I had been living for one year with a girlfriend whom I had met in Gothenburg when I started my studies at the Gothenburg College of Music. I was deeply in love with her, and when my father had his 50th birthday party, with all our friends and families gathered, we exchanged rings. Both of us seemed to be very happy.

A week later, she just disappeared and was gone for 10 days. I finally located her at her parents' house, where she told me she had fallen in love with another person — also a flute player. Needless to say, this was a real shock to me! The following year was a very turbulent phase in my life, with lots of parties and intensive social contacts, as I avoided being alone. I became very suspicious in my relationships with women and immediately backed off if the relationship seemed to last more than three hours.

After a year, I was offered a temporary job as principal flute player in the "Umeå Sinfonietta" and the "Norrlands Opera." This was in the town of Umeå, about 700 kilometers north of Stockholm. When I got there, alone, I suddenly had the opportunity to focus completely on myself for 18 months, reflecting over the last year's episodes.

I regained my motivation to be a top flute player, by simply deciding not to let the bad episodes in my life take away the things I could do better than many other people: playing the flute and engaging myself in music. During this period, I practiced extremely hard; 12 hours or more every day was not uncommon. The reward for this effort was given to me in 1989, when I applied for all five flute positions in the different Scandinavian orchestras, and was awarded all five!

The best reward was, of course, that I also matured as a person. Today I live with Maria and our 6-month-old daughter, having the time of my life, and all those crises are definitely behind me. I am working in the Royal Philharmonic Orchestra of Stockholm and in Benny Andersson's (ABBA) Band, and I record all kinds of music — Swedish folk music, pop, jazz, classical, improvised music, and so on — with the best musicians in Sweden.

William Bennett)))

William Bennett has received the Most Excellent Order of the British Empire for his distinguished service to music, as well as the National Flute Association Lifetime Achievement Award. In addition to his renown as an international soloist and recording artist, Bennett's worldwide masterclasses and professorships at Germany's Music Hochschule and the Royal Academy of Music in London have established him as one of the foremost flute teachers of the age. For more information, visit http://muslib.mmv.ru/wibb.

I got my first flute at age 12 — a thick wooden Rudall Carte. When I was 16, I went to the Guildhall School of Music and studied with Geoffrey Gilbert, who was "the man with the platinum flute." I didn't attach a great deal of attention to that — I didn't believe that flutes had to be platinum. But after I'd been studying with him for about a year, I went to a lesson one day and said, "I think I need a new flute."

He asked why, and I said, "I can't get the right sound out of mine in the top register." He said, "What is the right sound then?" And I said, "I have a record of the Paris Conservatoire Orchestra doing Debussy's 'En

Bateau.' And that's the right sound." He beamed and said, "Oh, well, that's good. That is Lucien Lavaillotte. He plays on a Louis Lot flute, and so do I." So I said, "I want one."

Subsequently, a couple years later, I heard Fernand Dufrene, one of my greatest idols on the flute, and he also played on a Louis Lot. But right after my talk with Geoffrey, I went out and found one which had been rebuilt in London. And after a few months I discovered I was having problems again — it was prodigiously out of tune.

All flute players tend to blame themselves for bad intonation. So I was blaming myself at first, when in fact it wasn't me — it was the stupid flute with all the holes in the wrong places. It had been rebuilt with too short a scale: B was flat, C was even flatter, and the E was sharp. What a mixture! I had to push various notes up and down, and much too much, to get them in tune. By the time I was 18, I was really struggling with this flute, having to bend myself inside and out to play it.

Then I went on tour of the States with my army band, the Scots Guards. When I was there, I tried a Powell flute, and I thought, "This has to be the most perfect thing I've ever tried — it seems to be in tune." (I've later gone back on that.) I made tracings of a Powell flute scale by pressing keys from a Powell down on paper and getting prints of where the holes were. The Powell C wasn't flat, so I got a knife and carved as much as I could out of the C hole of my Louis Lot. It was still flat, but not quite as bad as before. That was the beginning of the tuning business for me — it pushed me to do some work.

I bought an old Haynes made by Powell, and of course that was equally out of tune, but in the opposite direction. Where the rebuilt Louis Lot was as flat as a pancake on C, this thing was as sharp as 10 razors on the C, the B, and the C-sharp — and flat as something very rude on F, E, and all the notes below that.

So I was switching from one instrument to the other with completely opposite problems. The difficulties of dealing with these poorly tuned old instruments pushed me to develop my flexibility and pitch control. I found, after a certain amount of practice, that I could move some of the notes as much as a major third by opening and closing the mouth hole with my lips.

The flute has an inherent quality of changeability, which makes it more human than most of the other wind instruments. That's what I love about the flute. With your lips directly in control of everything over the mouth hole, you have the ability to change color beautifully and easily. But a flute is also a suit and should be made to fit you and your requirements. The problem is that most flutes are not perfect. People are superstitious and think their instruments have been made by gods, but Verne Q. Powell in Boston or Louis Lot in Paris were just ordinary, struggling people like you or me who were producing state of the art instruments according to the information at hand. Makers don't always want to listen to players who want something different, especially if they can currently sell more items than they can produce.

Flute players flagellate themselves when they can't get the right intonation, saying, "It must be me." But usually it isn't. Get the old hammer and chisel out and alter the flute until it suits you.

Jacob Berg)))

Jacob Berg has received the National Flute Association Lifetime Achievement Award and an Award for Distinguished Service to Music from the Peabody Chapter of the Johns Hopkins Alumni Association. He was principal flutist of the St. Louis Symphony Orchestra for 30 years, and has served as principal flute in the Buffalo Philharmonic, the Cincinnati Symphony Orchestra, and the Kansas City Philharmonic. He is former president of the National Flute Association.

The year before I retired from the St. Louis Symphony, I was diagnosed with lung cancer. I managed to make it through my last season, and then tried to continue playing in spite of treatment and its various unpleasant results. I was able to keep going for almost three more years.

Until recently, I played baroque flute with the Collegium Vocale of St. Louis, and last winter I was able to make a recording of Villa-Lobos's "The Jet Whistle" with my most musical friend Savely Schuster, former assistant principal cellist of the St. Louis Symphony. It's a beautiful and difficult piece, and it's very satisfying for me to hear it.

However, I've suffered neurological problems as a result of treatment that now make it very difficult for me to play. It's strange — when I'm sitting next to a student, I have the feeling that I could play the music I'm teaching. It's in my ear, it's in my fingers, it's in my mind. When I pick up the flute and find I can't do it, it's almost a surprise.

I still have reason to hope my ability to play will come back, so I'm practicing and teaching and doing the best I can. I've had an interesting career and played a lot of great music with a lot of great musicians. I feel fortunate, and I don't really have any regrets — except that I smoked.

I smoked for about 20 years. Though I quit back in 1970, I have been told that my cancer was probably caused by cigarettes. The most important message I can offer, not just to flute players but to all young people, is this: Do not smoke. Stay away from cigarettes.

Hope and optimism keep me going. It took this powerful event in my life to make me realize how much I love music and how much I love the flute. If things go well, that's wonderful, but this realization is a blessing regardless of what happens. I know that I will always get pleasure out of music.

Jean Berkenstock)))

Jean Berkenstock has been principal flutist for the Lyric Opera, Chicago, for 33 years. She is also former principal flutist for the Grant Park Symphony Orchestra and co-founder and member of Midsummer's Music Festival in Door County, Wisconsin. Berkenstock serves on the faculty of Chicago College of Performing Arts at Roosevelt University.

When I was in high school, I wanted in the worst way to get into the Chicago Youth Orchestra. I auditioned every year for a flute position, but there were always three or four girls ahead of me in proficiency. I auditioned again during my senior year, but I still didn't get in.

Three weeks later, the Chicago Youth Orchestra was holding auditions for bass violin. At my high school, there was a bass violin that no one ever used, so I took it home and taught myself to play it. I practiced the bass line from a hymnal, which was the only easy music I had for that instrument. I'd studied piano for many years, so reading the clef was no problem. On the day of the auditions, I went down there with my bow. There were probably 15 or 20 bass players auditioning, and they had us all stand across the back and play Mendelssohn's "Italian Symphony" along with the orchestra.

The conductor stopped the orchestra during the first movement, at a solo where the basses have to play way up high. He said, "Now we'll hear the bass players audition." One by one, we had to play that solo in front of the orchestra. When the selections were made, I got in — and I wasn't even the last one.

I went to rehearsals for the next three weeks, and after the third week the conductor asked me to stay afterwards. He said, "Jean, you really don't know how to play the bass, do you?" I said, "No I don't. Not really." And he said, "I've seen you here auditioning on the flute many times. You should be in the flute section."

So I got in that way. Often there are ways to your reach goal that you may not have considered, and you should be bold enough to try something different. It paid off for me in that case.

The final twist of all this was that I really enjoyed playing the bass. I played bass in the Evanston Symphony, which was an amateur orchestra, for the rest of my senior year, and I doubled on piccolo. When I left the symphony, the personnel manager said, "You were good on the piccolo, but we're really going to miss you in the bass section."

Emily Beynon)))

Welsh flutist Emily Beynon was appointed principal flute of the Royal Concertgebouw Orchestra, Amsterdam, at the age of 25. Alongside her fulfilling orchestral position, she performs regularly as a soloist both in recitals and with orchestras, and enjoys performing with various chamber ensembles. Beynon is a Fellow of the Royal Academy of Music, and students come from all over Europe to study with her at The Hague Royal Conservatory. For more information, visit www.emilybeynon.com.

Shortly after finishing my studies, I found myself in a somewhat depressing and rather overwhelming predicament. As both a performer and teacher, I strive, as I'm sure we all do, to heed the composer's every dot, dash, and word, and in doing so, to lift the dots off the page and convert them into tangible feelings, moods, and colors. The choice of every note and each harmony had a purpose in the composer's imagination, and it is our task to convey that to the audience through our chosen instruments.

But this meticulous attention to detail can at times become so intense and absorbing that, contrary to what we wish to achieve, we actually get led further and further away from the real "truth" of what the music is saying. That's where I found myself during this particular period — I was trying to be a clear pane of glass through which the thoughts, emotions, and intentions of the composer could shine through to the audience. But I began to feel like I was just spiraling deeper and deeper into searching for the sake of searching. By concentrating so intensely on all the nitty-gritty detail, I had lost all contact with my actual goal.

Fortunately, around this very time, I was invited to join a string orchestra playing all six Brandenburg concertos in Japan. When I got my passport back with my Japanese visa, I saw exactly what I needed to see to get myself back on track — "Purpose of visit: AS ENTERTAINER."

What would the millions of people who enjoy dancing do without music to which to dance? What would a taxi driver do were he unable to listen to the music on the radio? What would a film be without a music score? In playing or listening to music, we all respond on a very deep emotional level, and even in its most abstract forms I believe music is not a luxury, but rather a necessity in everyday life. At times, as we study every note and examine every harmony, it's important to keep in mind our real purpose as musicians.

Frances Blaisdell)))

Frances Blaisdell has received the National Flute Association Lifetime Achievement Award. She served as the first woman flutist for the New York Philharmonic and played for 15 years with the New York City Ballet. Blaisdell has taught masterclasses throughout the United States and in Venezuela, and toured China and the Soviet Union as a delegate for the National Flute Association. She has taught at New York University and the Manhattan School of Music, and currently teaches at Stanford University.

In 1928, I was 16 years old and graduating from high school. My father told me one day it was time to decide what I wanted to do with my life. "We'll see that you're educated," he said. "You may be a school teacher, a secretary, or a nurse. And if you can't decide, I'll decide for you. You can be a nurse."

I said, "No I couldn't do that. I'm going to be a flute player." He said, "You can't be a flute player because there's nothing you'll be able to do with it. I think girls should be trained to earn their living, and you couldn't make a living from playing the flute. So you can be a nurse."

At that time, not one woman anywhere in the world was playing in an orchestra. Actually, there may have been a woman playing harp in Philadelphia, but certainly nowhere else.

I talked to my mother, who was very understanding, and she convinced my father to hear me out. I said to him, "Most of the people in my class are 18, and I'm only 16. If I could be accepted into The Juilliard School, would you give me two years? At the end of that time I'll become either a secretary or a teacher — I couldn't be a nurse."

He said, "I don't approve, but I will give you the two years — and not another day. Do we understand each other?"

So I wrote to the Juilliard school and arranged an audition with the great French flute teacher there, Mr. Georges Barrere. When I arrived on my scheduled day, the woman in the lobby said, "And who are you?" I told her, "I'm Frances Blaisdell and I've come to play for Mr. Barrere." She said there was some mistake, and I thought she meant that I'd come on the wrong day. I showed her my letter, but she said, "Oh no, we expected a boy." Someone in the office had spelled my name "Francis" with an *i* instead of an *e*.

She said, "I'm very sorry, but every student accepted into this school is a potential professional musician. And there's nothing you can do as a professional — I'm sure you understand." I said, "I don't understand. Just because I'm a girl, I can't have an education?" I told her I couldn't go home and tell my father I didn't even audition. She gave in and said, "Well, the time has been reserved, you can go play for Mr. Barrere. But he won't take you, I'll tell you that."

With a very heavy heart I climbed the long flight of stairs to his studio. When he opened his door, I was terrified. Here was this man with a monocle and a long mustache with the tips waxed way up, and he spoke with such an accent I could hardly understand him. To make things worse, I hadn't brought a pianist, because I didn't know I was supposed to have an accompanist.

He let me play my solo all the way through, and then he looked right through me with those black, beady eyes of his. I didn't know whether I'd played well or not, or whether it was what he wanted. He said to me, "You go to ze office and you tell zem I want you. And if necessaire, you have full scholarship, comprende vous?"

I bounded down those stairs far differently than the way I had come up. In the office, they summoned the registrar. This was a critical moment for them — a crisis. She said, "Well, I don't approve. We've never had a girl wind player in this school." I didn't care what she thought or said, I was in.

That fall I had my first lesson, and I worked very hard for the following two years. But I always knew my father meant what he said about "not a day longer." At the end of the two years, I won Juilliard's concerto competition, and my father came to hear me play. After the performance I went to find him, and he was standing in the lobby. He looked very angry, very grim. He said, "I enjoyed it, but I didn't like it. I don't know what you'll ever do with this, but I have to let you finish."

I was elated. I just couldn't believe he'd go back on his word — he never had. And to think that I could go on studying my beloved flute was more than I ever dreamed.

Flute Stories

Wissim Boustany)))

International soloist Wissam Boustany has performed throughout Europe, Asia, the United States, and Latin America. He has been awarded a knighthood by the Lebanese government in recognition of his music and peace work. Boustany has made numerous recordings, including several solo CDs, and teaches at Trinity College of Music in Greenwich. For more information about Boustany or his international organization Towards Humanity, visit www.wissamboustany.com.

I was born in Lebanon in 1960. During my teen years, my country imploded into a very bloody 18-year civil war, as well as warring several times with our neighbor, Israel. When I left Lebanon to finish my studies in England, I put the war behind me and focused instead on my career and my love for the flute.

In 1991, several years after establishing a career as a touring recitalist, I fell into a depression. I lost my love for the instrument and could no longer understand the relevance of standing on stage, being applauded for an evening of flute music. It all seemed pointless to me. This period coincided with a lot of depressing world events — unremitting tension in the Middle East, as well as horrible wars in Bosnia, Rwanda, Iran and Iraq, and Chechnya. This sea of human misery reawakened my memories of the civil war in Lebanon. I realized I could not sweep my past under a carpet and avoid facing up to my experiences as a teenager.

In the process of dealing with this depression about the world and what my little flute could do in the middle of such futile reality, I realized that I needed to make some changes in my attitude. I had known early in my career that it was my love for the flute that drove my creativity and success. I discovered now, however, that in order for that love to stay alive, it needed to evolve. Loving my flute was not enough anymore. I needed to love humanity — to love life — and my love for the flute would have to be part of a bigger love that drove every deed and action.

I decided that I would fight back against cynicism, prejudice, and militarism with my flute. I would redefine the sounds that came out of my instrument to appeal to people's sense of compassion, love, and respect for life, and to reclaim some of the media's attention from the many wars that dominate our lives through the news. This idea evolved into Towards Humanity — an initiative to use music as a catalyst for raising funds and raising hopes in countries suffering the tragedy of war.

Since then I've raised close to $200,000 for humanitarian projects around the world. This work has helped me build the strong conceptual and emotional foundation that my music stands on. I realize now that every sound that escapes my lungs has the potential to move people and to make life better.

Love is a very, very big word, but it needs to be fed and to constantly redefine itself, otherwise it curls in on itself and dies. And without that in my heart, my flute is nothing; my life is nothing.

Randolph Bowman)))

Randolph Bowman is principal flutist of the Cincinnati Symphony Orchestra. Previously, he was a member of the Orpheus Chamber Orchestra and enjoyed a successful freelance career performing with New England's premier ensembles. He has premiered and recorded many new chamber works with Collage New Music, the contemporary music ensemble for the Boston Symphony Orchestra. Bowman serves on the faculty of the Conservatory of Music at the University of Cincinnati. For more information, visit www.cincinnatisymphony.org.

Since I started studying music when I was in college, I figured I was kind of behind schedule. At that point, I was told by a number of people that it might be too late to seriously consider a career in music. But when we're young, we tend to be headstrong about these things.

My very first audition was for a spot on the Boston Symphony Orchestra, and I finished in the final three. No one was chosen, but they liked my playing and I thought, "For my first audition, that wasn't so bad. This process is not as hard as I thought." Then I went through a period of taking auditions, and although I met with a fair amount of success, it seemed that I was always the bridesmaid and never the bride. I didn't want to go to a small town, so I only went to the bigger auditions. I was always runner-up, or one of the last three or four people — never first.

It took me another 10 years to win a principal job in a major orchestra. I was busy working all that time, but I began to realize that what I was doing was great for my 20s — when I got into my 30s I didn't want to have to do it anymore. A tenured job comes with benefits, and you don't have to constantly work so hard. My wife wanted to have children, and that was a big consideration. Being a freelancer, always on the road, wasn't so conducive to starting a family.

I tried out again for Boston. At the time, Boston was starting an eight-year run of auditions to find a principal flutist, and this was the very first one they held. After various rounds, it was down to myself and Robert Langevin, who at that point was still with the Montreal Symphony. We both played with the orchestra, but Seiji Ozawa decided not to give the job to anyone. For me, that was very discouraging. I had grown up with my musical education in Boston, and that was the job I'd always dreamed about. But Cincinnati came up soon afterwards and I decided to take that job and leave Boston.

In those days I had what they call the "fire in the belly." I just really wanted to succeed, and I had a grim determination to overcome the odds. But after being in Cincinnati for awhile, I reached the point many of us reach in our mid-40s — sort of a midlife crisis. It had to do with something that affects every musician in this business: To succeed, and to push yourself above and beyond the crowd, you have to be tremendously self-critical. But at the same time, you have to have the confidence to go out in front of 2,000 people and play. So you're constantly trying to balance this mixture of self-criticism and bluster. Unfortunately, a lot of people in this business don't find the happy balance, because it's psychologically very difficult.

When I was younger I loved the challenge of trying to conquer a very difficult piece, but as I got older, my innate professionalism got out of control. I set up such impossible standards for myself that I didn't enjoy playing anymore. It got to the point where I thought, "What else could I do in life?" People didn't believe me when I said I wanted to quit music, but it seemed absurd to spend my time practicing a piece over and over again only to mess it up in performance. It wasn't that I was really messing anything up, it was just a complete lack of perspective. Everyone else was congratulating me, and I was bitterly disappointed.

The inspiration that got me through came from the music itself. It finally dawned on me that I was performing music all the time, teaching music, practicing music, but I was never listening to music. So I put on recordings of my teacher, Julius Baker, which had had inspired me to play flute in the first place. Listening to this music that I really loved was invigorating, and it helped get me back on track.

I really do enjoy playing, and the funny thing is I feel much more relaxed about performing nowadays. I just had to get to the point where I could let go of the perfectionism and enjoy the process again.

Bonita Boyd)))

Bonita Boyd is professor of flute at the Eastman School of Music and former president of the National Flute Association. She is principal flute of the Aspen Festival Orchestra and has toured extensively throughout the world as a solo and chamber artist. She concertizes with famed guitarist Nicholas Goluses, and their debut CD as the Boyd-Goluses Duo was recently released by Albany Records. She has also released a collection of Paganini violin works, "24 Caprices" (Fleur de Son).

Whenever I used to feel low artistically, my lessons with Joseph Mariano were incredibly uplifting. Many times we played duets, and he would do amazing things musically that inspired me to think further. Then I'd leave the room, and within two hours the doldrums would set in again. I couldn't remember how it was that I was so inspired.

When this happened, Mariano would suggest I listen to recordings of great artists — not flute recordings, but people making music in other mediums. He would say, "Go listen to Dietrich Fischer-Dieskau," the great German baritone, or he might suggest the vocalist Elisabeth Schwarzkopf.

Listening to these people was life-changing. It was really about transcending the flute and becoming a musician.

One day — when I was very down, and thinking to myself, "Will this ever work out? What am I doing?" — Mariano looked at me and said, "Bonnie, do you believe in eternal life?" I remember being completely nonplussed because I was in my existential period at the time, so I said, "Well, I don't know." I'll never forget the look on his face when he said, "How, Bonnie, could you think that a great spirit like yours could just be extinguished?"

That was all he said, but I thought about those words for years.

Margaret Campbell)))

Margaret Campbell is principal flute with the Orchestra of the Royal Opera House, Covent Garden. She also has an active career as a soloist, appears regularly as guest principal flute with the major London orchestras, and broadcasts on BBC Radio 3 with pianist John Lenehan. Previously, she was principal flute with the City of Birmingham Symphony Orchestra. She may be contacted at windplayer@MargaretCampbell.co.uk.

I was offered the job of principal flute at the Royal Opera House in July, 1986. I couldn't start straightaway because I had to give three-months notice to the City of Birmingham Symphony Orchestra. I was going from a comfortable job where everybody knew me to a new job where I felt I had to prove myself, and I thought, "I've got to play fantastically here as I leave and even better when I get to the Opera House."

I'd always known my embouchure was slightly crooked, and I decided that perhaps if I played with my embouchure more central, I'd get a bigger, better sound. I tried to change it. Of course, it didn't work.

I went through agony trying to change the way I'd been playing for the past nine years. I was totally screwing myself up, but I couldn't let anyone know what I was going through. It's a difficult situation — who do you turn to with problems when you're already an established player?

I went down to London to start my new job, and at the first rehearsal, I remember thinking, "I don't know if these bottom notes will come out. They're going to know I can't play anymore." It was all in my head, really, because everyone was very welcoming, and looking back, the recordings I made during that period sound normal. When I had to produce the goods, I did. But it felt awful at the time, and I was really losing confidence.

I was on the verge of telling the Opera House that I wouldn't be able to do the job. In November, I was supposed to record a new commission for BBC Radio Three by John Mayer for flute, piano and tampura. It was technically quite difficult, and I thought, "I just can't do this. I'm going to tell them I can't play anymore." I rang the BBC office the evening before, but fortunately nobody picked up the phone. So I thought, "I'll have to go then," and I turned up for the recording. I went through total agony, but it came out fine and was broadcast as it was meant to be.

I then had to do an important concert performance of Shostakovich's Fifth Symphony with Bernard Haitink, and I thought, "I just have to get through this and it has to be good. It doesn't matter what my embouchure looks like." I realized I would just have to relax and blow wherever it felt right and sounded good. So I scrubbed the on-paper ideas I'd been messing about with and went back pretty much to where I was playing before. It went fine.

I realized then how important it is to trust your instincts. You can read an awful lot of books about the flute, but a lot of it may not be applicable to you. People use different means to produce the end results.

I look back now and I can't imagine what possessed me. No one sitting close to me had any idea what I was struggling with; if they had known, my confidence would have dropped even further. It was important for me to get through it somehow on my own, and I did — and 16 years later I'm still enjoying my job as principal flute for the Royal Opera House.

Flute Stories

Catherine Cantin)))

As a soloist and chamber musician, Catherine Cantin tours throughout Europe, the United States, Japan, and the former Soviet Union. She has been principal flute of the Orchestre de l'Opéra de Paris and performs with many of Europe's top musicians and ensembles. Cantin is an adjudicator for the prestigious Jean-Pierre Rampal competition.
Also a world-renowned recording artist, she was nominated for a Grammy Award in 1995 for best instrumental performance. She may be contacted at catherinecantin@wanadoo.fr.

In 1987, I participated in the Jean-Pierre Rampal International Flute Competition. I was very ill at the time, prone to fatigue and coughing fits that totally depleted me of energy. Jean-Pierre and many of my friends suggested I go see a doctor, which I did after the competition was over. The doctor informed me that I had tuberculosis, and that both my lungs were infected!

I rested for many months because I lacked energy, the illness having completely worn me out. I missed almost a year of playing in my flutist position at the Paris Opera as well as in solo performances and chamber music concerts. The most difficult part of this ordeal was not rediscovering my breath — the tests showed that I had a superior lung capacity despite my illness, probably thanks to all my prior playing — but trying to get my energy, motivation, and lip strength back.

I tried to put everyone's mind at ease by telling them that with discipline I would soon return to the musical scene. The most important lesson I learned was to keep faith in myself and to be patient — to accept the illness with wisdom, and then little by little to return to work. It was a challenging year, but one which greatly enriched my life.

Several years later, when I was pregnant with my second child (I have four children, two boys and two girls), I was invited to replace the solo flutist at the Paris Orchestra. Disaster hit when I started playing at the first rehearsal: I found that I couldn't hit G major, and that I could get nothing out of the lower notes.

I "rowed" through the first part of the rehearsal, then during the break I went to go see the conductor, Semyon Bychkov. I explained to him my regret at having to stop the rehearsal — he would have to find another replacement. He reassured me by saying, "I didn't hear anything wrong," but I told him it was out of the question for me to continue. Playing each note required too much effort.

I went to check out what was wrong with me, and it turned out to be hormonal. It seems that the "pregnancy hormone" — which facilitates flexibility and muscle relaxation, and is indispensable for giving birth — was very high in my system during the third month, and it affected my lip muscles! After about two weeks, I went back to work and everything was normal again. Bychkov didn't hold it against me, and to this day I am grateful to him.

These two stories illustrate that with patience and optimism, everything can be quickly put back into place.

Celia Chambers)))

Celia Chambers is principal flute of the London Philharmonic Orchestra, which she joined in 1982. She plays regularly at the Royal Festival Hall, London, and tours throughout Europe, the United States, Japan, and Australia. In addition to orchestral recordings she has released a solo CD, "The Lyric Flute." Celia Chambers holds an appointment at the Royal College of Music, London. She may be contacted at hctaylor@onetel.net.uk.

My mother grew seriously ill when I was a student in London, and she died during the first term of my second year. I was 18 — shy, insecure, and full of anxiety — and I felt utterly lost. Though I had some wonderful friends, at a deeper level I was unable to unlock my feelings to anyone.

However, looking back, this was a very significant growth period for me. It triggered a huge amount of creative energy, longing, and a desire to reach somewhere hitherto unknown to me. It was then that I started to really focus on my sound, practice carefully, think, and use my imagination.

Several years later, as my career began to take off, I went through another time of soul-searching. I was busy with a lot of work in London, and meanwhile my husband and I were trying to raise two daughters. I felt that I was not playing the flute properly, nor was I being a good mother. I joined the London Philharmonic when the girls were 7 and 10, and this ambivalence continued. London orchestras have a punishing schedule, and one has to pace oneself very carefully, taking time off to recover, rest, and rejuvenate. I never found an answer to the problem of playing flute and raising children, except that one just has to do what one has to do.

My daughters are both delightful adults now, and I'm very proud of them. As for the LPO, we recently performed Bach's St. Matthew Passion at the Royal Festival Hall with Kurt Masur, our principal conductor, and it was an example of music-making of the highest order. I felt, and continue to feel a tremendous sense of privilege that I am part of the London Philharmonic.

Flute Stories

Herbert Ascherman, Jr.

Kathleen Chastain)))

Kathleen Chastain teaches flute, chamber music, pedagogy, and professional development for musicians at the Oberlin Conservatory in Ohio. She has appeared in solo and recital performances in the United States, Europe, South America and Asia. She released a solo CD with French pianist Laurent Boukobza in 2003.

I was in Jean-Pierre Rampal's class at the Paris Conservatory, and it was a very difficult time for me because I had two children. Women get tied up emotionally in their children, and in my moments of fatigue my heart was going out to my kids and not to my music. They felt my tension as well, and whenever I had an audition or something important, one of them would fall sick.

It got to the point where I really wanted to stop playing, and the person who kept me from quitting was my husband. He said, "No way, you can't stop. You have to keep going, even if it's a little bit. If you do stop, you're going to regret it later on." My colleagues in Paris were also very supportive, and I love them all — especially my husband, Michel Debost, who was also a colleague.

So when my children were small, I decided to do less. I taught lessons at home, and I did a few gigs, but not too many. As they grew up, I was able to do more and more, and for me that was wonderful.

I have a lot of female students, and they're often asking me, "How did you do it? Should I have kids? Should I not have kids?" And the first thing I say to them is, "Get a husband who's intelligent, and who won't say, 'Why don't you stop playing and take care of your children.'"

Flute Stories

Ann Cherry)))

Ann Cherry's versatile career includes work as a soloist, recording artist, writer, editor, and arranger. She has performed with numerous orchestras and ensembles in Europe and the United States, and founded the Academia Wind Ensemble, which includes some of England's finest players. She has published arrangements of Bach flute sonatas and French-related show pieces for flute. Cherry served on the faculty of Trinity College of Music for 28 years. For more information, visit www.fluteconnection.net/contfl/contfl.html.

I always took music for granted. My parents were professional musicians, and I guess I just assumed that I would be a musician too. Well, in truth, I never really thought about it at all. It just happened.

I mostly attended the Cleveland Institute of Music, where I enjoyed myself immensely. I got on well with my teacher, Maurice Sharp (who gave me many extra lessons); I held first chair in the orchestra and the opera orchestra; and I was much in demand for ensemble work. I ushered at Severance Hall and so heard the Cleveland Symphony for free every week. I was even paid to usher for the children's concerts! And I was expecting to graduate very near — if not totally — at the top of my class. What could possibly go wrong?

Well, I was run over by a car. Hit and run; the driver was never found. I suffered a lot of injuries — serious leg fractures, and my head was split open — but to me the most worrying thing was the loss of my two front teeth. I was convinced I would never be able to play the flute again.

This belief was strengthened when I tried to play my flute — the cheapest model Armstrong — with no front teeth. I sounded awful! It was the first time in my life that I had to face the possibility — no, the probability — of not being a musician. That was when I realized how much the flute meant to me.

But my parents were wonderful; they had faith where mine had disappeared. They had placed an order for a new Haynes flute, and they didn't cancel the order after the accident. My new flute arrived at almost exactly the same time as my new front teeth were fitted. And can you imagine the joy of playing that first note, with teeth, on my new silver Haynes?

The memory of that moment, the realization that I *could* play again, inspired me to practice hours and hours, and to enjoy practicing with a new understanding. My injuries forced me to remain with my parents for the next year and a half, but I had further help and inspiration from Murray Panitz, who gave me some lessons, and who was wonderfully patient and encouraging.

It's funny how what appears to be the worst ill-fortune can actually be a blessing in disguise. I received a little insurance money through my parents' automobile policy, which I used to go to London and study at the Royal Academy of Music. This led to my moving to Rome and having lessons with Severino Gazzelloni; to my becoming heavily involved in new music; to my return to London as my permanent residence; and to my subsequent career in chamber music and solo performance. It's all rather spooky, really. None of these things would have happened if that car had not run me down.

Flute Stories

Chris Lee

Sandra Church)))

Sandra Church has been associate principal flutist for the New York Philharmonic since 1988. Previously, she was principal flutist of the New Jersey Symphony and the Chautauqua Symphony. She has recorded chamber and orchestral music for Sony Classical, Cala Records, Musicians Showcase Recordings, and Teldec. For more information, visit www.newyorkphilharmonic.org or contact her at churchs@nyphil.org.

When I first decided to attend Juilliard, I had no concept of what I was getting into. The curriculum in education is more comprehensive these days for students embarking on a performing career, but I just approached everything as it came. I loved to sing in high school and college, and I was drawn to the flute partly because it's a soprano instrument, a real voice. Playing the great classics of the orchestral repertoire was a moving experience, and I was amazed by the idea that I could be paid for it.

I went on to Juilliard after attending Syracuse University, and it was a revelation to me how much there was to learn. Beginning a serious study is an enormous undertaking — it all seems so huge. There's a great deal of specialization when you get to that level, and even though I was actually interested in a lot of things, I was inspired to become very focused and specialized. Discipline, patience, and learning to be on time became good habits, and I also enjoyed the camaraderie of my school colleagues.

I got my bachelors and masters from Juilliard. It's a strange sensation when you finally get a master of music degree. You think to yourself, "OK, I'm a master of music. What now?" Even though I came out of this big conservatory, I was suddenly on my own.

I knew I didn't want to freelance — I always wanted to play in an orchestra. As a matter of fact, I always wanted to play for the New York Philharmonic. But around the time I graduated, I started taking auditions and learned what a tough, tough process it is. Part of it is matching the right person to the right orchestra. You've got to have the right sound, the right temperament, the right depth to your playing. It's also about having faith in your own preparation.

I kept thinking that somewhere, some orchestra would want me to play flute. It wouldn't be every orchestra, but it would be somewhere. No matter where I was performing, there would be artistic growth.

Getting a job in the New Jersey Symphony was a very lucky break. They had an open audition, and when I tried out, the music director, Thomas Michalak, gave me the opportunity to be principal flute. It was thrilling. Finally I had my own chair and concerts to play.

Attaining a position gives you confidence. You have new responsibility and you can express yourself as an artist. I find the life of a symphony musician to be rich and satisfying — a blessing indeed.

Flute Stories

Tadeu Coelho)))

Dr. Tadeu Coelho is professor of flute at the North Carolina School of the Arts. He has performed as first solo flutist of various orchestras, including the Santa Fe Symphony, Hofer Symphoniker in Germany, and the Spoleto Festival Orchestra in Italy. As an avid proponent of new music and Latin American music, he has commissioned, performed and recorded works by many notable composers. For more information, visit www.ncarts.edu or www.miyazawa.com/artists/tadeu_coelho.htm.

As a student in New York, I never believed I could be a good teacher. My original plan was to be an orchestral player.

My wife and I had come from Brazil to study in the United States. We decided we wanted to stay in the U.S. after graduation since we loved this great country. I took several auditions, I applied for jobs, and I was getting nowhere even though I was practicing six or seven hours a day.

We were here initially on a student visa, and consequently we were expected to go back to Brazil. I had invested great efforts on my training and I believed I had the ingredients to be a good candidate for a job here

— I went to the Manhattan School of Music and I had studied with wonderful teachers such as Julius Baker, Ransom Wilson, Keith Underwood, Thomas Nyfenger, Andy Lolya, and Arthur Ephross.

One day I went to an audition for the San Antonio Symphony. I called up a Brazilian friend in San Antonio beforehand and asked if I could stay with him. He told me to come on a Friday so we would have some time to catch up, and he added, "On Sunday we'll go to church." Going to church didn't seem too much of a price to pay for a free stay. Little did I know, my life was about to change drastically.

That Sunday turned out to be a very important one — I think God really spoke to me, to my heart. On Monday I took the audition. I didn't win, in fact I didn't even go on to the second round, but I learned something very important about my life: My priorities were all wrong. I went back to New York a changed man. I told my wife that something was missing in our spiritual lives. She suggested we go to her friend's church in the Bronx — Manhattan Bible Church.

It was a scary experience, and the people there seemed really strange to us at the time. As the pastor got up to preach, he mentioned that all of his friends from his youth had been either murdered or killed in prison. Other people shared their testimonies: One had been a prostitute and lost her children, others had been on drugs but were now free. These changed lives made a strong impression on me, though I was reluctant to commit at first. I told my wife, "I'm not going to go to a church where the pastor is an ex-drug dealer." My wife kept attending, however, and she would share with me every week the many wonderful lessons that helped us answer the questions about our own lives and the problems we were having. I finally decided to go back.

I felt led by the Holy Spirit to give my life to Christ, and I accepted

Him as my Lord and savior. This really changed my life. It was the most important thing that ever happened to me.

Right after that, the professional doors opened to me. I was offered a job in New Mexico as a flute teacher. This was particularly testing for me, because I had always planned to be an orchestral player. Nonetheless, I was thrilled and took the job, which made it possible for us to stay in the U.S. To my amazement, I found out how much I love teaching — how much I cared about my students and learned with them every day.

I owe much of what I learned about teaching to a wonderful person whom I met in New York: Ronald Roseman — a Jewish oboe player who became a believer in Christ through playing the works of J.S. Bach. He passed away a few years ago, but his influence lives on the lives he touched. He showed me how to care deeply for each student, and if there is any humanity in the way I teach now, it is due to him.

As students, we learn to make plans, but sometimes what we end up doing is different from what we were initially hoping for. I've been teaching and performing extensively for over 12 years, and I just love it. My wife and I are becoming U.S. citizens, and we are so grateful that this country has adopted us. I have no words to express the gratitude that I feel for what God has allowed me to do. We make the plans, but it is God who blesses them.

Robert Cole)))

Robert Cole has received the National Flute Association Lifetime Achievement Award. He played principal flute with the Philadelphia Orchestra for 13 years. He has also played in the Wingra Quintet, the Madison Symphony, and took part in TV broadcasts and recordings for Columbia Records with the Philadelphia Woodwind Quintet. Cole is professor emeritus at the University of Wisconsin-Madison, where he taught for 27 years.

I would never have gotten into music at all if it hadn't been for the local school loaning me a flute and pointing me in the direction of a flute teacher. By the time I was in sixth grade, I'd had about two years of piano, and it didn't take at all. In fact, my dad was so disgusted that he said he'd never pay for another music lesson for me.

But the school band needed a flute. My older brother played the violin, and since he could read treble clef, the band director asked him to take the flute home. I picked it up and was able to blow it, so my folks decided that maybe I should play flute. The band director told my parents that we could use the instrument if they saw to it that I had private lessons, and he recommended a teacher.

There were lots of musicians working in movie theaters just before the Depression, but when the "talkies" came in, the theaters just gave up their orchestras. These guys were out on the street, in effect, and had to start teaching to make a living. My new teacher and his wife had been theater musicians, and they were both good to me. When I was supposed to have an hour-long lesson, I'd have an hour and a half. We'd play Kuhlau duets, and if I had to be in a solo competition, his wife would play the piano parts for me during my lessons.

After high school, I got accepted to the Curtis Institute of Music, but at the end of my first year they closed down the wind department because of World War II. I had to go into service like most guys my age. I knew I wanted to be a professional musician — I loved music — and I decided that if anything happened to my fingers during the war I would start playing French horn.

I spent three years not playing much at all. After the war was over, Curtis said everybody could come back. If you don't play for three years when you're 22, you have to do a little practicing to get back into it. But William Kincaid was a fine teacher and very understanding. I got married, and my wife worked for the next three years while I was in Curtis.

I took a few auditions and got accepted as second flutist in New Orleans. They sent me a contract for $60 a week for 20 weeks, and I wrote to them, "Can't you do better than that? My wife is expecting a baby, and I make more money than that teaching in Philadelphia." And they wrote back, "Good luck in your hometown."

So I went home to Erie and finished my college credits. That fall I got a telegram from the Philadelphia Orchestra saying one of their older flutists, John Fisher, had had a heart attack and wasn't coming back right away. Would I like to sub? And of course, since I didn't have a regular engagement, I said yes. I performed with them for several months, and by March it became clear that Fisher wasn't coming back. They told me my internship was over and made me a permanent member, and that was the beginning of a very fortunate career.

Flute Stories

David Cramer)))

David Cramer is associate principal flute for the Philadelphia Orchestra and a former member of the Montreal and Pittsburgh symphonies. He has participated in the Tanglewood Festival and the Central City Colorado Opera Festival and is a frequent chamber music performer in the Philadelphia area. He has served on the faculty at Carnegie-Mellon University and currently teaches at Temple University in Philadelphia. For more information, visit www.philorch.org

I studied in high school with William Hebert, who was piccolo player with the Cleveland Orchestra, and a great teacher as well. He was everything I needed at the time — a well-rounded teacher who was good at explaining technical things. Then I went to the Curtis Institute and studied with Murray Panitz, and at first I went through a problem adjusting.

Murray had some different ideas about the right way to do things. He certainly knew what he was doing, but he wasn't as interested in discussing technical issues. He was more of a coach. He would tell you to do things without explaining them down to the last detail.

One thing he wanted me to change had to do with the relationship of the lips to the embouchure plate. Murray wanted me to cover much less of the opening, to develop a more "open" sound. It's a crucial relationship, because if you cover too much you end up with a more squished, nasal sound. If you open too much, you can lose the center to the sound — it can be too "hooty." And it becomes much more difficult to play soft, and to control intonation.

Murray had said to cover less, which I did. Then I'd go to my wind ensemble, where my teacher was John de Lancie, the famous oboe player. His big thing was to play soft — he wanted us all to have the control to play very quietly. I was having a lot of trouble playing soft, because I was going overboard with Murray's instructions. It sounds so simple now, but back then it wasn't obvious to me at all. These kinds of technical changes are all in terms of millimeters, and it takes a lot of experience to know exactly what effect a change like that will have.

I felt like I was getting conflicting requests from two important teachers, and I wanted a little help. So after my first semester, I went back and played for William Hebert. I told him, "I'm having all this trouble. Murray Panitz wants me to do it this way, but it's not sounding so good."

Hebert just looked at me and said, "Well, don't do it so much."

I remember almost laughing. It was so simple — and it was an important lesson for me. I just needed a little perspective. And when I got back to Curtis, Murray was certainly happy with the adjustment I made. He never said a thing about it.

Flute Stories

Gareth Davies)))

Gareth Davies is principal flute with the London Symphony Orchestra. He enjoys working in schools as part of LSO Discovery, convincing young people that you don't have to be old or boring to enjoy classical music, and is in demand as a visiting professor in most of the London music colleges. Previously, he played with the Bournemouth Symphony Orchestra. His debut recording of the Nielsen Flute Concerto is available on Naxos.

I started playing the flute at the age of 10 after seeing this Irish guy — I forget his name — on a children's TV program. He had a gold flute and said it was easy to play. That's the instrument for me, I thought.

I played for fun and never practiced much, as I was too busy with rugby, soccer, and swimming. I joined the local youth orchestra and had great fun playing music with friends. I can't remember making a conscious decision to become a musician — it just sort of happened that I found myself auditioning for the London music colleges. It was the first time I had come across the likes of William Bennett on a panel, listening to me make a mistake on the first note of the Faure Fantasie. I didn't pass that one.

I ended up at the Guildhall School of Music and Drama in London, where I had several different teachers. Up until this point, I had been taught by Evelyn Frank, who to this day has had the biggest influence on my playing. She was a former pupil of Marcel Moyse, and she taught me about color, phrasing and the importance of the music and its meaning. I loved her approach to music — it was so different to anyone else's.

In college I was bombarded by technical studies, scales, and exercises, which were of course vitally important to improving my fairly relaxed attitude to the technical side. I was upset, however, to learn that my embouchure was very unsymmetrical. I hadn't really noticed before, but I was blowing out of one side of my mouth. I was told this was unacceptable; as I progressed it would be inflexible and leave me with a smaller palette of colors than other players. I had always considered that my range of colors was one of my strong points, but you can't argue with your teacher — not in your first term, anyway.

So for the first eight weeks of the year I stood in a practice room with a mirror and a headjoint, trying to straighten my embouchure. As the weeks passed, I sounded more and more like a Peruvian panpipe player and I lost all flexibility. I seriously thought about giving up. I was even asked to go to a British Flute Society teachers day as a "model" to demonstrate the perils of uneven embouchure. "So you see, Mrs. Smith, if you don't sort out your daughter's face now, she will surely sink to the depths of this poor unfortunate creature, and crawl around the dark recesses of the London underground playing 'Annie's song' to tourists for eternity." At least that's how it felt.

Everybody seemed obsessed with making my face look right but ignored what sound was coming out, which seemed to be missing the point. Gradually, the teacher began to lose interest and gave up tying to change me. By this time I had stopped bothering and reverted back to my old embouchure. I figured that nobody has a symmetrical face, and just because somebody, once upon a time, said that you had to blow from the center of your lips, doesn't mean I have to. So I didn't.

I'm now principal flautist in the London Symphony Orchestra and my embouchure still looks a bit odd, but it works for me and you can't spot it from the audience. The only people who ever notice are conductors, who sometimes give me a funny look — but don't get me started on that one!

As Frank Sinatra said, "I did it my way," and it works for me.

Philippa Davies)))

Philippa Davies performs and broadcasts throughout the world. She is a popular BBC Proms guest since her acclaimed 1988 performance of Mozart's D major Concerto. Her schedule includes many world premieres; numerous distinguished composers have dedicated works to her. She also performs with the Nash Ensemble and London Winds. Her recordings, from Mozart to Ligeti, are bestsellers. She teaches at the Guildhall School of Music. For more information, visit www.gsmd.ac.uk, or contact Davies at flute@pipdavies.freeserve.co.uk.

Six years ago, my husband died. My life was very much intertwined with his because he was a composer, and his music was — and still is — a very important part of my life.

I met Paul Reade in 1988, when I was asked to play his flute concerto, which he'd written in 1980. I fell in love with his music, fell in love with the man, and then we got together, so the whole thing was a very involved musical relationship as well as a close personal one.

In 1996 he was diagnosed with lymphoma cancer, and tragically, a year and a half later he died. Obviously, when something like that happens, you reevaluate everything. So much was gone from my life, I wasn't sure what was left. Because of his music, and because of my relationship with the flute and love of music in general, I was very fortunate and I was able to struggle through. In a way, this was what kept me going and alive.

I had a sense also that I wanted to keep his music alive. The wonderful thing about composers is that they write their music and it's there forever. And it's an added joy if you're married to a composer, because they start writing things for you. There was a piece he had arranged for me that always made me cry when I played it, even when he was alive. It still makes me cry — there's a wonderful freshness about it.

I'm planning to record his flute concerto this year, which would have been his 60th birthday. I feel strongly that's something I can do for him — play his music. It is now six years since he died, and one's life changes, but he's very much there in my memories and in his music. His music will always live on.

Timothy Day)))

Timothy Day is professor of flute at the San Francisco Conservatory of Music. He spent 12 seasons as principal flute with the Baltimore Symphony and taught at the Peabody Conservatory. Day has served as acting principal flute of the Minnesota Orchestra and the Boston Symphony, and has performed with the San Francisco Symphony, Opera and Ballet orchestras. He is an active performer in the motion picture recording industry.

Learning the flute was generally not difficult for me, but there came a time when I seemed to reach that "last frontier" as a student, and I grew frustrated technically. I'd play difficult pieces like "Firebird" and the "Classical Symphony" over and over again, and sometimes I'd nail them. Then, the next time I played them it was like I'd never seen them before.

At one lesson with Robert Willoughby, I went in ready to play Hindemith's "Acht Stucke." There's a passage consisting of triplets that go way up into the stratosphere and then come down again. I was determined to nail it, but I totally crashed and burned. I was about ready to throw my flute through the window, but he said, "Wait a minute — play it again up to that point to where you start breaking down. Find out where the initial problem starts."

When I figured out exactly which note it was, he said, "Write a tenuto on that note." He also had me write tenutos on several notes before and after it, then said, "Try the passage again. When you get to the difficult part, play deliberately under tempo and play tenuto on every one of those notes that you've marked."

So I did, and afterwards he asked me, "Well, what do you think?" I said, "I got all the notes, but the hard part was completely out of tempo." Willoughby played back my performance on a tape recorder, and I freaked out — all the triplets sounded absolutely smooth and in tempo.

And he said, "What happened was, you forced your eyes to slow down and see what you were playing *while you were playing it*. We all read ahead to some extent while we're playing. When you come to a difficult, dense passage, the message to the eyes become garbled. They don't want to focus on all that information, so your eyes just run ahead down the page and you end up trying to play based on some kind of muscle memory. What you just did was pull your eyes back and force them to watch the notes in real time.

"By fooling yourself, thinking that you're playing slower, what you're also doing is counteracting the effects of adrenaline and what it does to your sense of real time."

That was an incredible lesson for me. You have to have a clear visual picture of what you're playing as you're playing it. Using this new tool, within a week, all those pieces that were giving me fits were now accessible to me. And it was no longer necessary for me to go over everything two hundred times in order to play it right.

Ever since Willoughby showed me that method 30 years ago, I've been using it as one of my everyday teaching techniques. It's one of those things that works every time, and it's bailed me out of some really intense professional situations.

What it all boils down to is this: If you can see it, you can play it.

Flute Stories

Michel Debost)))

Michel Debost has received the National Flute Association Lifetime Achievement Award. He teaches at the Oberlin Conservatory in Ohio, and previously performed for almost 30 years with the Orchestre de Paris. His new book, "The Simple Flute" (Oxford University Press), is available through Flute World at flutes@fluteworld.com

During the '50s, I served in the French army in Algeria. This experience compared to what young American men lived through in Vietnam, with the same end result — defeat and casualty. I stayed there for two years without playing the flute, and I thought I was all washed up. Nowadays two years seems short, but when you're 20 it feels like forever. Morally and musically, I felt totally worthless, and I almost took a job working with helicopters.

But an old peasant friend of mine, in Dijon, said he was sure that playing the flute was like riding a bike: you never forget. And it turned out he was right. I gave myself another six months, and when I started playing it came right back. I began getting gigs and won a few competitions, and soon I was making a living.

I still tell my students: Never quit completely. Even if you must stop temporarily, keep playing, and whatever you learned before will come back to you.

Flute Stories

Priska Ketterer

Robert Dick)))

Robert Dick is a creative virtuoso in the tradition of Paganini and Hendrix. Composer, performer, improvisor, author, teacher, recording artist, and inventor, he is known worldwide for redefining the flute. His compositions are performed by flutists around the globe and he's received numerous grants and commissions, including a Guggenheim Fellowship, two NEA Composer's Fellowships and a Koussevitzky Foundation Commission. He is visiting professor of flute at the University of Iowa. For more information, check out www.robertdick.net

When you take an independent pathway as a musician, you have to weave together a lot of financial threads. There is no single thing I do which supports me, and I've had only a few short periods in my life where things were financially easy. From early on, I did whatever I could to make money, from playing and teaching to gardening. Somewhere in my mid-twenties, I did what I declared what was my last nonmusical job.

I had a wonderful position lined up that summer to be a tape editor, but it fell through at the last minute, and I was forced to take the only full-time job that was left through the student employment office — at the Yale-New Haven Hospital morgue.

During every autopsy, a set of tiny samples are taken from the body and put in a 2-liter jar filled with formaldehyde. A piece of tape with a number is put on the lid. Over fifty or sixty years, Yale-New Haven had accumulated thousands of these jars, and they were hopelessly out of order. They decided to hire a student to take them all out, put them in order and put them all back, so that if they needed jar #12,310, they'd know where to find it.

That student was me. Actually, I was an ex-student at that point. I stretched the job out as long as I could, and my immediate employer, who was an embalmer, was really sympathetic. He figured anyone who stayed on the job must really need it.

That summer I learned a lot of valuable lessons about time, and most of all about wasting time. When you see someone younger than you lying there dead, you can't help but learn huge lessons. Reality itself is your teacher. I remember my last day, as I walked out of there into the light of a blazing New Haven August, I said, "That's it. I'm never going to do anything again for money which doesn't involve music in some way."

And I haven't. That was a signal moment for me, and even though I knew how tough it was going to be, I was determined. Like Orpheus, I'd been down to the underworld. I'd spent a summer in the basement of the morgue. I just thought, "If I'm not going to emerge from there, I'm not going to emerge." Courage is being frightened going forward, while cowardice is being frightened going backward. Either way you're frightened, so you might as well go forward.

And it sure has been tough the whole way, but it's definitely been worth it. I was not put on the planet this time around to be a follower. I used to absolutely hate putting on those servant's clothes and going to the gig, and I never really liked following a conductor. I've worked toward the goal of being able to play the music I want to play, and only the music I want to play. For the last 17 years I've played solo concerts, primarily of my own music, and been a part of creative groups like the "rough jazz" A.D.D. Trio, the "ambient/overdrive" band King Chubby, and the "lyrical, modal" music of my duo with multi-instrumentalist Jaron Lanier and my trio with violinist Paul Giger and percussionist Satoshi Takeishi.

That's not to say my path is the right path for other folks. And I'm not trying to disparage anyone who loves playing with classical ensembles or playing with a conductor. The important thing is that we do the things that are true to us.

Louise Di Tullio)))

Louise Di Tullio played flute and solo piccolo for the Los Angeles Philharmonic before becoming a freelance recording artist for TV and film, recording for such noted composers as John Williams, Jerry Goldsmith, John Barry, and many others. She is principal flute of the Pacific and Pasadena Symphonies and the Hollywood Bowl Orchestra, and has taught at the University of Southern California, Cal State Fullerton, and the Music Academy of the West in Santa Barbara. For more information, visit www.pacificsymphony.org

As far as having a career in music, I don't think there was ever any question. I was born into two musical families. My dad, Joseph Di Tullio, and one of my uncles were both cellists with the Los Angeles Philharmonic, and my father had a brother who was a cellist and another who played violin. On my mom's side, I have two well-known horn players as first cousins: Vincent DeRosa and Henry Sigismonti. So there wasn't too much hardship getting my career going, except that as a young woman entering the field in the 1960s, I wasn't always taken seriously at first.

My dad gave me a great deal of my training. He also helped me through the crises of being really young in an older person's professional world. And many times he gave me the strength to stand up to people.

I won my job at the L.A. Philharmonic at a time when it was going through management changes, and Georg Solti was supposed to be director that year. I was 19, which is pretty young for the philharmonic. The following year, I was joined by several other young players — Michelle Zukovsky, Dave Breidenthal, and Barbara Winters — but the first year I was kind of alone. And that was a tough place to be. There were some politics in the flute section at that time which made it difficult for me.

I was hired on as associate principal but I wound up trading jobs and playing piccolo. I remember one European conductor coming to town to be guest conductor for the orchestra. He walked into rehearsal, saw me there with a piccolo in my hand, and looked me over strangely. Then he had the orchestra turn to the third movement of the Bartok Concerto for Orchestra. He singled me out and said, "You play."

When I was younger I had played on a youth orchestra under a tyrant who screamed all the time. Thanks to that, as well as the training from my dad, I was able to keep my cool. I picked up my instrument and played. After hearing me, the guest conductor paused, then said, "Now do it this way." So I played it again the way he asked. This went on several times — each time, he'd stop me and order me to do it a different way.

Finally, he turned back to the orchestra and said, "Good. Well, gentlemen, we can begin." And I remember hearing the loudest gasp from the orchestra, because they knew what he'd been trying to do. But I guess I passed the test.

Aralee Dorough

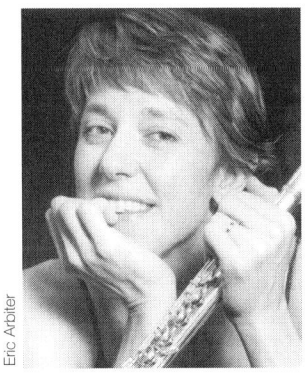

Aralee Dorough)))

Aralee Dorough is principal flutist of the Houston Symphony. A frequent soloist with the orchestra, she recorded Mozart's Concerto in G and performed the premiere of Bright Sheng's "Flute Moon." With the Houston Symphony Chamber Players she has recorded and performed chamber music in Europe and Japan, and at Chicago's Ravinia Festival, often with Christoph Eschenbach at the piano. She can be contacted at editor@www.upbeat.org. She recently recorded on the new UpRite vertical flute: www.homecookedCD.com.

It was my fifth year playing second flute in Houston and I'd decided I wasn't happy with it. I wanted to play principal somewhere and was taking whatever auditions became available. Still, deep down, I had doubt as to whether I could handle the pressure of a first flute job.

We had recently gotten a new music director, Christoph Eschenbach, when our principal flute chair became available. There was electricity in the air because we were all excited to be working with him. I realized that this principal job, out of any orchestra in the world, would be my dream job.

I prepared the best I could ... but I lost the audition. Although I played one of my most accurate auditions ever, I didn't get into the finals. I was crushed. But a few weeks later, when the committee didn't give the position to anyone, I knew there was a glimmer of hope. I decided to talk to Eschenbach. He was an intimidating figure, so serious and intense, and I'm usually quite reserved, but I just had to know how he perceived my audition, and I had to let him know how much I wanted to work with him. He took out a small black leather-bound book and gave me comments from his notes. He said my playing was not interesting enough.

I said to him that I knew I could make a better impression playing *with* the orchestra. Could I have one week to prove myself? He didn't say anything, but the next day I got a call from the general manager asking if I'd be interested in playing "acting principal" from June through May! I knew what a huge opportunity this was.

When June arrived, the first repertoire I played was Shostakovich 5 and a Chopin piano concerto. It was just an afternoon concert with an insignificant conductor, but I imagined my every move would be scrutinized. At the rehearsal I was tense and didn't play well. I was thinking negative thoughts, thinking I didn't have any right being there. At the concert I had a full-blown case of performance anxiety. I was nearly paralyzed by the idea that I might play a wrong note. When the Shostakovich started, I was filled with dread for the beautiful, soaring solo coming up at the end of the movement.

But soon the gloominess of the music made me think of my teacher, Tom Nyfenger, who had died unexpectedly the week before. When the music became angry sounding, I began to feel angry — angry he was gone, angry I was feeling so nervous. Soon I was playing with anger, and I was no longer tense and locked up. When the solo came, I simply played it — an offering to Tom. It was no longer a matter of being a good or bad player.

Getting through that concert was the first step in what lay ahead that year. Some of the best repertoire of the season went to the candidates who were being considered for the job. I was not considered an official candidate. But I kept working hard and didn't allow myself to be upset. As the year went along I learned to bring my playing forth from that emotional place: anger, grief and joy. I learned to enjoy the thrill of what we call pressure — to play the best you can under extreme demands. Eschenbach was a big influence in that direction. He knew how to make you go beyond your safety zone and succeed.

In March I got to play Brahms's First Symphony in Carnegie Hall. It was the turning point for me getting serious consideration for the job. The last piece I played that season was Mahler's "Das Lied von der Erde," which has two big cadenzas with vocalist. The flute part is simply marked pianissimo, but I knew Eschenbach would want more shading and drama. It had to be sensational, but also make sense in the context of the piece. I studied the score and experimented with every possibility of shape and tone color.

When I played it in rehearsal, I knew I'd hit my mark. Most importantly, I had come a long way since the scary Shostakovich of 11 months earlier: Every time I played that Mahler solo, it was a thrilling, enjoyable experience. I knew there was nothing else I'd rather be doing.

A week later I was offered the job, and after twelve years, I still love it.

Flute Stories

Elena Durán)))

Elena Durán's successful concert career takes her throughout Europe, the United States, Mexico, and South America. She has appeared frequently on television and has hosted her own radio programs in the U.K. and Mexico. Durán taught at the Birmingham Conservatoire in England and is now artistic director of the annual International Flute Festival in Stratford-upon-Avon. She has made numerous recordings and has a series of books published by Schotts. For more information, visit www.fluteconnection.net/contfl/contfl.html

Because of the way I grew up, for many years my general belief system was based on fear. Later, I got to the stage where I decided, why not base it on positive thinking? That change in mind-set, and my ability to self-validate, helped me overcome and accomplish everything I wanted to do with my career.

As a flute player, being first-generation Mexican was never a problem for me in itself. I was never treated any differently. But psychologically, I had to overcome the duality of having a very Mexican home life and a very American education. I grew up in Oakland, California, riding the bus every day with Latinos and blacks to an American school, and yet I spent weekends doing things like going to Mexican movies in Spanish with my grandma.

I learned how important it was not to be insulted by people who are naïve. For example, because I played a musical instrument, I'd sometimes be told, "You don't act like a Mexican." I wasn't insulted, because I didn't think those people knew what they were talking about. I thought Mexicans could make great music.

But there were other things to overcome, and those included coming from divorced parents and having a mother in the hospital who was very schizophrenic. I visited her on alternate weekends, and sometimes she'd had shock treatment. That was difficult. I didn't talk about it with friends until I got older, because I didn't know what context to put it in. They could go see Jack Nicholson in "One Flew Over the Cuckoo's Nest," but it wasn't really like that. It was worse.

The important thing, I discovered, is the ability to self-validate. Musicians often feel very insecure, and if we don't play well one day or aren't chosen at an audition, we don't feel validated. But it's important to remember that everybody's been in those situations — everybody famous. I was incredibly lucky in that I was able to study with Jean-Pierre Rampal. He said, "Even the really great artists have really great failings." You're not going to have the best performance every time. It's a matter of being able to live with that. If you validate yourself first and somebody else doesn't, you're still going to be okay. But if you're waiting for somebody else to do it, there's going to be trouble.

I learned to take what was around me and make it a vehicle for positive thinking, whether it was a friend, a recording, or learning something new. I also began to focus on the people around me who were very confident.

Most importantly, I have a really great marriage. Michael Emmerson has been both my husband and my partner, and he's the best thing that could have happened to me in my adult life. As my mother says, if I ever get mad at Michael in front of her: "How can you be angry with the person who has given you the wings to fly?"

Does that mean I'm always positive? No — nobody can be like that. But I know how to overcome my negative side, and I know what's important. Whether or not somebody likes my flute playing is not really important, because any one person's opinion of you will not stop you from doing what you want to do.

When I was in San Francisco in 1966, I went to the very last Beatles concert, and I said to my cousin, "One day I'm going to meet Paul McCartney." I had to wait about 15 years but the call eventually came and I made a hit single and a video with him.

That's about the most positive thing imaginable. That is the ultimate belief in one's self.

Moshe Aron Epstein)))

Moshe Aron Epstein combines a solo and chamber music career with the position of flute professor at the Hochschule Academy of Music and Theater in Hamburg, Germany. He has been solo flautist of the Israel Sinfonietta. As soloist and conductor, Epstein has worked with most Israeli and numerous European orchestras, including the Berlin Symphony and Slovenian Radio Symphony Orchestra. He has published a practice book, "Mind your Fingers" (Zimmermann Edition). For more information, visit www.maepstein.de.

I was born in Israel, to a Jewish family who observed the Shabbat very carefully, including not being allowed to play any musical instrument on the holy day. When I was 9, I began playing flute with the Youth Symphony Band of our village, and I soon encountered a severe problem — a concert was announced on the Shabbat.

The conductor, who was a great teacher and musician but a most difficult person, knew no compromises. He refused to release me from that concert, saying that all orchestra members were needed. My parents and others tried to explain why it was impossible for me to play that day,

Flute Stories

but nothing helped. The conductor was stubborn and extremely secular in his belief. My flute belonged to the orchestra, and should I not appear in the concert, he threatened to take it back from me. Which he did.

All of a sudden, I found myself without music. I was devastated. My family was completely poor, like many other families in Israel at that time, and could not dream of buying an instrument for me. The question "how could a thing like that happen to a Jewish child in the land of the Jews" was bitter and hard.

My mother worked at a chocolate factory owned by another very hard and stubborn person. But he apparently was also warm-hearted. After hearing what had happened, he could not hide his anger at the evil which was done to me. He immediately opened his purse and offered my mother a big sum to buy me a flute.

My aristocratic mother accepted his kind offer under the condition that it was given to her as a loan. A huge calculating machine was brought to our home, and my poor mother worked on it each evening for four hours, five days a week for two full years. This was on top of her full-time job at the factory and managing a home with three children. She bought me a very nice old wooden Rudall & Carte flute, and believe it or not, I returned with it to the orchestra. The conductor became "softer" and accepted the compromise that I would be released from any concert, should it happen on Shabbat.

A year later I received my first solo — a transcription of Henry Bishop's "Lo, Hear the Gentle Lark" for flute and clarinet duet, plus orchestra. After several performances in our village came the big, great, most important concert at the Ohel Shem Hall in Tel-Aviv. How nervous we all were — and so was my flute. Shortly after the piece began, in front of a full audience, the thumb lever of my flute broke into two parts and fell on the stage. I stood helpless while the orchestra and the clarinetist went on playing (and praying, probably — even the conductor). After several seconds, I ran to the first flutist, took his instrument, and played on until the successful end of the solo.

No one in Israel knew how to adequately solder a broken flute in those days. After two years of running back and forth to all possible repairmen in the country, I was told "this flute is no more to be repaired." I was 12 years old but capable of working. I convinced the bank in my village to give me a small loan, which allowed me to buy a most horrible metal flute. Today it would be considered unplayable.

Over the years, I have had the pleasure of buying and playing several excellent flutes. Five or six years ago, I saw a wooden Rudall & Carte for sale, and it brought back warm reminiscences from old times. I bought the flute, and upon returning home I decided to open the box of my old "dead" R&C, which had not been touched for more than 30 years. It was horrible — all metal work was broken and springs pointed in all directions. A wreck!

I showed it to a friend of mine, Marten Root, when he was visiting Israel. Amazed, he looked at me and said, "This flute is *perfect!* You have to understand, it must have been produced in the 19th century, when hard, silver soldering was not applied. Therefore, all metal parts are not broken, only dissolved. All soldering can surely be redone."

Marten gave the flute to a wonderful repairman, Ton Kooiman, in the Netherlands. Two months later, my wife and I were in Amsterdam. Mr. Kooiman brought the repaired flute with him to our hotel room, and I was astonished at the beautiful instrument. It was like new, and played with a warm, beautiful sound.

With tears in my eyes I opened the curtains, so my late mother could see from heaven that *her* flute had returned to life.

Flute Stories

Andy Findon)))

Andy Findon is one of London's foremost session players, recording for TV, film and albums on a regular basis. Recent recordings include the scores for "Chocolat," "Star Wars (The Phantom Menace)," and the "Harry Potter" films. He was acclaimed for his solo flute playing in Andrew Lloyd Webber's new musical production "The Beautiful Game" and has played with all the London orchestras and many chamber groups. For more information, visit www.andyfindon.com.

When I was 13, my brother died. He was 15 and a true prodigy — on clarinet, piano and as a writer. As one may presume, the atmosphere at home ceased to be so openly encouraging in music for a long while.

I, however, continued to play the flute and went on to Music College. Though I became principal flute in the National Youth Orchestra, I was never a successful student or "competitive" flautist, winning no prizes or great accolades. It wasn't until I began working and enjoying the company of professional musicians in all types of music that I felt at ease and fully confident in my playing.

I've just spent a week sitting in front of the greatest trumpet section, recording the music for a new James Bond film, and I regularly play with other woodwind players for whom I have such great respect and affection. Any personal problems I go through are overcome in order to not let them down.

I've been fortunate in having a good flow of work and a great social life around playing. And I know of nothing I would rather do than play.

Flute Stories

Davide Formisano)))

Davide Formisano is principal flute for "Teatro alla Scala" and "Filharmonica della Scala" in Milan, Italy. He enjoys a growing career as soloist and chamber musician, performing with many prestigious orchestras throughout Europe and Japan. He previously served as solo flute for the Hamburg Filarmonisches Staatorchester and the Netherlands Radio Philharmonic Orchestra. Formisano is an active teacher and recording artist. For more information, visit www.davideformisano.com.

I entered the world of highly competitive flute playing when I was only 16. Though I felt the music was wonderful, I found that what lay behind it wasn't so easy. Young musicians in particular are always in competition — they have to prove their abilities, sometimes successfully, sometimes not — and often they envy each other. Like any profession requiring constant performance, difficulties and discouragement were always waiting around the corner.

Whenever I found myself discouraged or faced with a problem, I never let the experience remain negative. I've always wanted to see the naked truth, to try and face it, to stay focused on solving it. By doing this, I've had to admit that I *have* difficulties, which is not so easy for anyone to accept. But it's the only way I know how to solve problems. Discouragement can be positive. Being aware that even troubles can help me has always inspired me to continue.

I come from Naples, in Southern Italy, and the people of that city have a motto which is a bit rude and vulgar, but which in my opinion is very centered on this issue. They say that to obtain anything, you must have the three C's — *cuore, cervello,* and *coglioni. Cuore* (heart), means dreaming about what you want to do. *Cervello* (brain), means being sharp enough to understand which way you should run. *Coglioni* (literally male attributes, which stand for strength and resistance) means staying true to your path, without paying attention to negative people who discourage you.

Discouraging moments are quite common in a musician's career, and I've had my share like anyone. But if you really want to reach the top, you can't lose yourself in difficulties. Time is never enough — you have to rise up again and again, to struggle and obtain what you want.

Flute Stories

Taffi Rosen

Patrick Gallois)))

Patrick Gallois enjoys a highly successful international career as soloist, recording artist, and conductor. He performs frequently with major orchestras throughout Europe and in Asia. He has made more than 60 recordings, including 10 on the DGG label. Since creating his own orchestra in Paris, "l'Academie de Paris," Gallois has been invited to conduct orchestras around the world. He has been appointed Musical Director of the Sinfonia Finlandia in Jyvaskyla. For more information, visit www.patrickgallois.com.

As a soloist, I've had so many great experiences in my musical life. Sharing music with audiences and other musicians in a different country every week is the greatest thing in the world. Like other soloists, I've also faced some difficult moments and funny situations.

I remember being in Japan to perform the Mozart concerto in G major in Bunka Kaikan, Tokyo's big concert hall. During the performance, I began to improvise my cadenza. At this period in my life, Mozart's G major concerto was not my favorite one, so I began to play one element of a theme from Mozart's concerto in D major. Then I realized that I had forgotten which concerto I was actually playing — G major or D major — and I didn't know how to end the cadenza.

While I was playing, I kept trying to look around at the conductor's score to see which concerto it was. But Jiri Belolavec, the Czech conductor, saw what I was doing and thought he was distracting me, so he kept moving the podium farther away.

A less funny situation occurred on my 30th birthday. I was in northern Holland performing with the Frisland Symphony Orchestra. It was one of those days when everything goes wrong: my flute was not working, the conductor was bad, the orchestra wasn't great either, it was raining, my new Jaguar wouldn't star, and I'd finished all my books and had nothing to read. My 3-year-old daughter Sophie called me to wish to me a happy birthday, and it made me so sad to think, "What am I doing out here?" Soloists often feel that way — alone and far away from the people we love.

It's a difficult time to be a soloist. At the age of 28, I had played seven years with the Orchestre National de France and two years in the Lille Orchestra, when I quit. I wanted to discover what it meant, for me, to be a musician. As a flautist playing on a modern instrument, I had nothing to do. These days, all baroque music is played on original instruments, and every country has one specialist who performs all contemporary flute music.

So I decided to begin at the beginning: Telemann wrote so much music for flute that I made an effort to interpret his music using a modern approach. I read books about him and other composers of that time — Quantz, Hotteterre, C.P.E. Bach — and used my knowledge of harmony and counterpoint to understand my instincts. I lose myself in Telemann's music because I had to find my own unique way of playing it. Strangely, this approach to Telemann helped me to work with new music as well, and to create many concertos working directly with the composers.

The next 10 years were a dream. I really grew to understand why I wanted to be a musician, and what I wanted to do with my flute and my musical life. My wish for all musicians is that they could stop everything, to take a period of their lives and work just for themselves, as I had the chance to do.

James Galway)))

James Galway is regarded as both a supreme interpreter of the classical flute repertoire and a consummate entertainer whose appeal crosses all musical boundaries. Through his extensive touring, over 50 best-selling RCA Victor albums, and his frequent international television appearances, James Galway has endeared himself to millions worldwide. For more information, visit www.superflute.com.

*L*ast year at a check-up it was discovered that both of my heart arteries were blocked up to over 80 percent. After the end of my U.S. concert tour I had surgery and received two bypasses. Since then I have changed my lifestyle to "diminuendo" and my nutrition to vegetarian — with the result that I lost weight enormously and I now feel like new.

The heart surgery was a sign for me that I am no longer up to the concert tour stress. Only the circumstance that I have extremely low blood cholesterol saved me in the past year from a heart attack.

However, I still feel that I am in such good shape physically, as well as psychologically, that the thought to resign has not arisen. If one day I feel that I cannot get the tone to sound as I want, or that the breath no longer cooperates as wanted, I will stop immediately. I definitely will not wait until someone tells me: Jimmy, I believe it is time to stop.

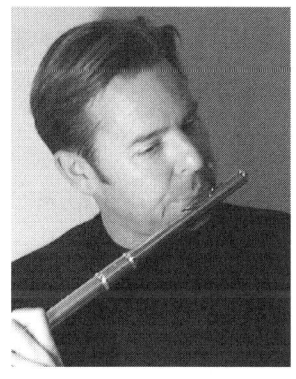

Bradley Garner)))

Bradley Garner is professor of flute at the University of Cincinnati College-Conservatory of Music, The Juilliard School, New York University, and Queens College. He has been principal flutist with the Atlantic Sinfonietta, New York Virtuosi, and Virtuosi Quintet, and has an active career as a soloist and recording artist. He has performed numerous times with the New York Philharmonic. For more information, visit www.cincyflute.com.

My parents were my original inspiration in music. They instilled a love for music in me and my two brothers, and all five of us played the flute, though not all professionally.

So much of what I know about playing the flute I learned directly from my dad, Gary Garner. I was lucky enough to take lessons with him every day from the time I was 12, although I didn't always think I was so lucky at the time, because when I was in 6th grade I was sure I knew more than he did.

I studied with my dad up through college, and he's still among the flutists I admire most. As I got older, Julius Baker became a huge influence, especially when I studied with him at Juilliard. Even now, not a day that goes by that I don't think about those two guys when I'm teaching. Two other players who have greatly influenced my love for the flute are Jean-Pierre Rampal and James Galway. I talk about all four in my teaching and think about them in my playing, trying to incorporate different ideas from each.

I think it's very important to have heroes, and not only flutists. I always tell my students, you've got to have a hero string player — maybe a great violinist like Jascha Heifetz — and a hero soprano, such as Cecilia Bartoli. We need to listen to these singers and violinists for ideas about things like vibrato, colors in sound, and releases of notes. Those things are inherently difficult on the flute, so without outside influences we often pick up bad habits and accept bad releases, or notes that are a little out of tune.

As flutists, we're so lucky to play the repertoire that we play. I look forward to going to work every day, trying to instill my own love for music in my students, sharing what little I know about playing the flute in hopes of making them better players themselves. I've got one of the best jobs in the world.

Laura Gilbert)))

Laura Gilbert has performed around the world as a soloist and with many musicians, ensembles, and orchestras, including the late pianist Rudolph Serkin, the Bach Aria Group, Musicians from Marlboro, and the Brentano and Saint Lawrence Quartets. She has made numerous recordings and is a member of the award-winning ensemble Aureole. Gilbert has taught at a number of schools, including Harid Conservatory, Mannes College of Music and Peabody Conservatory. She may be contacted at Legflute@aol.com.

I play in a trio called Aureole, and for almost every concert we play, we're asked to do Debussy's Sonata for Flute, Viola, and Harp, which is one of the big cornerstone pieces of 20th century chamber music. It's always been one of my favorite pieces of music, and I never tire of it.

After years of playing it, however, I finally did some research. I started reading up on Debussy, some of his letters and biographical material. I found out that he wrote this piece at the very end of his life, and that in a way, it was his musical last will and testament. I got this unbelievable fire under me — these incredible revelations about what this piece really was and where it came from — and then played about ten performances of it in a row, and it was like a completely new piece.

The inspiration I drew from this experience relates back to two anecdotes that I tell my students all the time. The first is about Ronald Roseman, the great oboe player who grew up in a Jewish Brooklyn family. When he played Bach's St. Matthew Passion for the first time, he became obsessed with it. He studied it, analyzed the score, and just lived with the piece. And because of that experience, he ended up converting to Catholicism.

The other story is about flutist Sam Baron, who was my first teacher. He was lying on his deathbed, fading in and out of consciousness, and his wife noticed that he was conducting something. She asked him, "What are you doing?" He said, "I'm thinking about Bach."

These anecdotes tie in with the deep connection that comes with interpreting music, and living with it. When I learn something new about a piece of music that I've lived with for a long time, it can be an incredible revelation. It's like discovering a new room in your house or a completely new personality trait in the person you're married to, or in one of your children. When the music exposes itself on all these different levels to me, it opens me up to new feelings about what it evokes and how I want to play it. For me, those are the most inspirational moments.

Scott Goff)))

Scott Goff has been principal flute for the Seattle Symphony for 34 years. He has been principal flute of the Mostly Mozart Festival Orchestra at Lincoln Center in New York for 19 years and was previously assistant principal flute for the Pittsburgh Symphony. He may be contacted at ptflute@yahoo.com.

I never practiced the flute much in high school. Things came readily to me, and once I got to a certain level I didn't go any further. I wasn't really interested in having a big career — I was interested in playing the flute and playing great music. My revelation came the summer after I graduated and went to study with William Kincaid. I was impressed with Kincaid and enjoyed my lessons with him, but I was still getting up my courage to make a commitment to the flute.

At that time, Julius Baker was playing with the Vermont Chamber Orchestra. I was this kid from the West Coast who'd never really heard him before, so I went to hear Julius play the flute. It was an epiphany — I had never imagined that an instrument could be played so beautifully, and at that moment I knew what I needed to do. As far as work, I realized I had a long way to go, but I finally made my commitment and started practicing hard.

A couple years later I ended up studying with Julius at Juilliard. I was so blown away, and still am, by the high level of the man's playing — his conception — and I wanted to emulate that. Of course, over the years I've moved into my own conception, but I've fought very hard to stick to what Julius showed me in terms of an absolutely musical and classical approach to the instrument. My primary interest is how I sound — a conception of tone, of rhythmic perfection, of purity of technique in which a minimum of fingerings are used. I've never flagged in that interest.

Julius threw down the glove for all of us when we were students, just by the way he played. To a large part, I measured up, and that is an achievement of which I am proud.

Bernard Goldberg)))

Bernard Goldberg has received the National Flute Association Lifetime Achievement Award. He is Principal Flute Laureate of the Pittsburgh Symphony Orchestra, where he was principal flutist from 1947 to 1993. Goldberg, founding conductor of the Three Rivers Young People's Orchestra in Pittsburgh, conducted the McKeesport Symphony and teaches at Brooklyn College, City University of New York. He has recorded on numerous labels. He may be contacted at bgflute1@juno.com.

In 1952, I was in the town of Prades, France, practicing for the Geneva Competition. I didn't end up entering because I ran out of money and had to return home to earn more by playing concerts. But in any case, as I was practicing, I felt very discouraged. I thought, "What's the use? Perhaps I'm not really a great musician."

This was during the Cold War, when there were perpetual difficulties between the United States and the Soviet Union, and it seemed so trivial practicing my daily exercises. I went to visit the musician and philosopher who had drawn me to that town, Pablo Casals. I told him how discouraged

I felt and asked him, "Why should I continue to be a flute player?" I thought maybe I'd do more good just standing on a street corner, telling people to throw away their atomic weapons and make peace.

As for my flute playing, I said, "I'm no Pablo Casals, I'll never be. I'll never have that enormous talent." I wasn't flattering him, I was just telling him what I felt to be true. I asked, "Should I give up the flute?"

He said, "No, no." Because of the condition of the times, I needed to continue playing — to play always — because music is a peace-making effort. "We need more music, not less," he said.

So, I went back down the street into my room and started practicing again, this time with the courage to say, "Yes, this is necessary. People may regard it as frivolous, or say, 'Who needs it?', but if I play Beethoven, Mahler, and Debussy well, it's a very worthwhile activity."

I believe that our music validates the human spirit. When Casals played the cello, you knew you had to do something better with your life and with the world situation. I had felt until that point that when Bernard Goldberg played the flute, it didn't mean anything. After all these years, my career has shown that maybe I was wrong.

Erich Graf)))

Erich Graf is principal flutist of the Utah Symphony. Previously, he performed with the New York Philharmonic, the New Jersey Symphony, the Royal Ballet Orchestra, and the Stamford Symphony, among others. He performs in recital with keyboard artist Ricklen Nobis and has appeared as soloist with various orchestras and chamber ensembles. Graf is president of Local 104-AFM. His discography (on the Aeolus label) include two CDs and a music video. For more information, visit www.erichgraf-flutist.com.

One of the great virtues of training with Julius Baker is that the musical aesthetic and standard you inherit is very high. But it also means there's no excuse for anything except success. At Juilliard, the focus toward a professional life in music is very strong, and in a large way, your success as a musician is determined by how successful you are in landing jobs.

I graduated with a pretty strong sense of a musical aesthetic in terms of what I wanted to do, though not knowing quite so well how I wanted to do it. I was moderately successful in New York as a freelancer, and I played with a wonderful group called the Aeolian Chamber Players for six or seven years. But over that time I learned that the flute players I respected most were usually the products of a lot of orchestral discipline. So it became a priority for me to gain the experience and the discipline that comes from playing in an orchestra.

Those of us who cope with the audition process learn that it's a baptism by fire. I took 14 auditions before I got a job. It was tough keeping the repeated frustrations from becoming a barometer of my self-worth.

What it boils down to is having patience and perseverance. At that particular time in my life, I had a strong will to succeed and refused to take "no" for an answer. I just kept trying, over and over again. Waking up the next morning and persevering toward that next audition, that next trial — that's a high-stress thing, but the rewards are immense.

I don't think we're in this profession by accident. Being an artist is sort of like having a carrot dangling out in front of you: You don't ever really reach the carrot — that point of pure aesthetic gratification — but that's a good thing, because you're always reaching for something better. There are other things you could do that would leave you more stable as a person. The artistic lifestyle is erratic at best, and it's not the world's most relaxing way to live, but then there's the excitement we have as artists when we create something that wasn't there before.

I wouldn't trade it for anything. One of the greatest pleasures I get in life is getting up in the morning, taking out the instrument, and seeing if I sound better than I did yesterday.

Peter-Lukas Graf)))

Peter-Lukas Graf enjoys international renown as a soloist and conductor. His concert tours and masterclasses take him all over the world, and he has released almost 30 recordings on the Claves Records label as well as many recordings for television and radio. He has conducted many prestigious orchestras and is author of three didactic monographs for the flute: "Check-up," "Interpretation," and "The Singing Flute." Graf lives in Basel, Switzerland. For more information, visit www.peterlukasgraf.ch.

At the age of 13, I had my first success with a Mozart flute concerto. I was flattered, of course, but I had already built up my own ideal of musical expression — perhaps by listening to my mother, who was a singer. Because of this, I felt strongly that my flute playing was not good enough, nor was it really satisfying. Any string player seemed to me more expressive, and I was envious of the much richer pianistic repertoire. These feelings had decisive effects on my musical life.

I didn't actually draw my inspiration from flutists, but mainly from musicians like the great cellist Pablo Casals, for whom I had the opportunity to play when I was 16; from singers like Elisabeth Schwarzkopf, whom I had seen in a Mozart opera; or from Edwin Fischer, with whom I played Brandenburg Concertos. I'll never forget Fischer's second movement of Bach's F-minor concerto — I tried for a long time to achieve with my flute the wonderful melodic expression of this pianist.

In my early 20s I began to play flute recitals with piano or harpsichord, as well as solo programs. The concert organizers thought I was crazy because this was unusual, at least in Switzerland. They were afraid to bore the public. But I had ambition and wanted to present the flute not as a virtuoso toy, but as a means for making music like a violinist or a cellist. For me, it was the greatest compliment to hear from people that during the concert they had forgotten they were listening to a flute player.

I compensated for what I felt was a lack of great flute repertoire by conducting. This was my main job for many years. My idols were Furtwängler, Klemperer, and Keilberth, among others — not to forget Eugene Ormandy who proposed me to succeed Kincaid in the Philadelphia Orchestra. I've often been asked which I prefer, conducting or playing? My answer is that while I am playing my hobby is conducting, and while I am conducting my hobby is playing.

Nowadays there is a new challenge for flutists: the "authentic" interpretation of old music. Two little stories show how much the world has changed. I remember a comrade who told me during our studies in Paris, "Bach is not difficult." Decades later, after a recital in Amsterdam which included baroque pieces, a colleague admired my "courage" for having played Bach on my Boehm flute in the metropolis of specialists! I try to approach music — including old music — as independent as possible of the instrumental means.

As a young orchestra player I had a nice old Louis Lot flute. But its pitch was about A339, and the orchestra's pitch was A443. I cut the head joint, and one can imagine all the problems this created. Today, flutists are in a luxurious situation, having numerous excellent flutemakers making perfectly scaled instruments with all sorts of specifics. We even have our choice of many different materials. This progress is impressive. But to some musicians and students who are mainly occupied by discussing which head joint or material is best, I say: Forget silver, gold, wood and platinum, and think more about music!

It was probably my early dissatisfaction with the flute that motivated me to search continuously for greater means and greater musical expression. My enthusiasm for exploration led me to love the flute as my personal instrument. It is important to have an ideal, and to keep it alive. We seldom reach it, but as musicians we have a great privilege — to be always on the way.

Flute Stories

Matej Grahek)))

Matej Grahek is principal flutist of the Slovenian Philharmonic Orchestra. He performs as soloist with the Slovenian Philharmonic, Big Band RTV Slovenia, and in various chamber groups both at home and abroad. He is a member of the flute quartet FOReM. Grahek records for the Radio Slovenia music program and recently released a solo recording, "Opus di jaZZ," for which he received the Slovenian Grammy award "Zlati petelin." For more information, visit www.sgn.net/mgrahek.

When I graduated from the Ljublijana Academy of Music, I didn't know what to do with my life. I was very lost. Should I teach in a music school? Should I quit the flute? There is a big limitation on what musicians can do in Slovenia, because we are a very small country, and at that time there were no openings for principal flute players.

I decided to go to Irena Grafenauer — she's also from Slovenia and teaches at the Mozarteum in Salzburg. She held an audition for about 40 flutists, out of which she picked five to study with her, and I was one of them. The two-year period that I studied with Irena was the most fantastic thing that could ever have happened to me. Not only is she one of the best flutists I've ever heard, but as a person she's fantastic and very open-minded. I learned so much about the flute during that time, and my confidence grew a lot stronger.

After two years, just like in a movie, there was an opening for the principal flute position in the Slovenian Philharmonic. I decided to do the audition, along with 15 other flutists. There were three rounds. In the first we played a Mozart concerto, and one of the jurors held the opinion that another flutist was better than me. But the jury decided to select me as well, and just the two of us were picked to advance.

In the second round I played a Frank Marten ballad. When it was over, I was alone going into third round, and some people were angry that the other flutist had not advanced. But in the third round I played solo parts with the orchestra, and after that the jury was united. I had won the audition.

Even though it's been six years since I became principal flute of the Slovenian Philharmonic, I can still say that was the most exciting day of my life.

Flute Stories

Marco Granados)))

A Grammy-nominated performer, Marco Granados has received worldwide acclaim for his diverse flute repertoire, dynamic sense of rhythm and exhilarating style. In addition to his work as a soloist, he has toured with several renowned ensembles, including the Quintet of the Americas, Triangulo (www.triangulo.org), and his own ensemble Un Mundo. He serves on the faculty of The New School in Manhattan. For more information, visit http://sunflute.com.

I grew up in a small village in the mountains of Venezuela, where there was no way to study a musical instrument. There were no music teachers, and music wasn't being offered at the high school. My dad wanted my brother and I to learn how to play an instrument, so he tried taking us for lessons to the capital of our state, an hour away. It was such an ordeal that he got it into his head to start a music school in our hometown.

He did a lot of fund-raising, from both the private sector and the government, to provide for teachers' salaries. Somebody donated a house we could use, and then the National Orchestra of Venezuela donated instruments. Within a year and a half, my dad was actually able to start his music school — and it was free for the kids in the town.

My dad told us, "You can learn two instruments," and I said I'd start with the piano. He asked what other instrument I wanted to learn, and the word just popped out of my mouth: "Flute." I remember the reason I chose it was not because I particularly wanted to play the flute, but because I didn't want to play the violin, which was the instrument my dad played. I just didn't want to be following in his footsteps. So I began taking flute lessons.

At the beginning, I showed a lot more talent for the piano than I did for the flute, but this goes to show how incredibly important a good teacher is in one's creative evolution: My piano teacher was an old, uptight German lady. My flute teacher, on the other hand, was a kind man who played in the state concert band and drove out from the state capital to teach us. He would stay late, way beyond the allotted lesson times, and tell us stories of things he'd done, of performances and so on. That really inspired me, and so I put a lot more effort into the flute.

Three and a half years after I had begun playing, I heard about an opening for second flute in the state concert band. I don't know what got into my head, but I decided I wanted to try out. I practiced something like six hours a day during my entire summer vacation, and when I showed up for the audition, I won the job.

My dad was shocked — he wasn't expecting me to win. And here I was, this 13-year-old kid with a professional job. The salary came out to something like $1,500 a month, which in those days was a nice amount of money. My dad worked out a deal with me — he'd let me take the job as long as I used my earnings for education.

The way my career has developed has definitely not been the norm for most flute players. I've been presented with unusual choices along the way, and I've had the opportunity to explore many different types of music. But what I find so exciting about the flute, and about a life in music, is the opportunity we all have to continue learning and evolving throughout our lives. If we remain willing to try different things, we can always find an open door to a whole new process of learning.

Marc Grauwels

Marc Grauwels is one of the world's best-known flute soloists, with more than 50 recordings to his credit. He played first solo flute for 10 years with the Belgian Radio and Television Symphony Orchestra and played solo piccolo for the Belgian National Opera Orchestra. Grauwels recently signed a deal with Naxos to release a series of about 30 CDs called "The Flute Collection." He teaches at the Mons Royal Conservatory. For more information, visit www.marcgrauwels.be.

One of the most difficult things to learn, when you first start to make recordings, is how to stand in front of a microphone and make music with no audience. When I did my first recording with the Belgian Radio Symphony Orchestra, I was nervous going in. I was so obsessed by technique — determined that my performance would be technically perfect — that I let the personality in my playing be pushed to the side.

This is typical for a lot of students and people getting started in the professional world. Younger players often try to be perfect, 100 percent. They listen to other flutists and imitate their sounds, trying to play beautifully using perfect technique. I had to learn during my first recording sessions — the most important thing is that the *music* is there, not just the technical part of it.

Something about recording goes against the true nature of music, and that's what makes it stressful. When you play a concert for an audience, they inspire you. The music and the emotion belong to that moment, and make that moment magical — and then the music disappears. It doesn't stay. When you record, you're trying to keep it and make it stay. Maybe it's for humanity or for the future, maybe for pretentious reasons.

In the studio, I discovered how important it was to tell myself that I was not in a studio. By imagining I was in a fantastic concert hall, and by visualizing the people out there hearing my performance, I was able to condition myself to make music. Once I understood this, I started to really enjoy making recordings.

Susan Greenberg)))

Susan Greenberg, a member of the Los Angeles Chamber Orchestra, has performed with many prestigious ensembles, including the Los Angeles Philharmonic, Hollywood Bowl, and Los Angeles and New York City operas and has played at the Casals, Ojai, and Martha's Vineyard Festivals. She has played principal flute on many film, television, and commercial recordings, including "The Lion King," "Far From Heaven," "The Simpsons," and the Warner Brothers cartoons. She may be contacted at Susanflute@aol.com.

I was an only child raised in a home where I was expected to be quiet, and I wasn't allowed to express myself. Music was my outlet. It came really easily and I loved it. For someone who was to be "seen and not heard," music allowed me to be "heard and not seen."

I excelled early. In the sixth grade I was already playing flute as first chair with the seniors. But I loved the piano, which was my first instrument, and I played both instruments all the way through high school. When I was in 10th grade, I was playing first chair flute with the Northern California Honor Orchestra, but I auditioned with the orchestra to play a

Flute Stories

piano concerto. A few weeks after the audition, while out to dinner with my mom, we found ourselves seated next to the conductor and he actually talked to me. This was a big deal — I was just a kid! He said, "You know, pianists are a dime a dozen. I think you should concentrate on the flute."

That one moment really changed my path. The next day I called up a flute teacher who was in the San Francisco Symphony, and I started getting really serious. By the next year I won to solo with the Oakland and San Francisco Symphonies.

When I graduated from high school I chose to major in music, but it didn't occur to me that I could perform for a living; I thought I might teach. I was only 16 when I got to UCLA, and the first year that I was there, the principal flutist in the L.A. Philharmonic, George Drexler, asked me to play a concerto with him in a program. I remember that we got a really good review, and I thought, "Maybe I could do this."

Over the next few years, a number of things happened — I won first chair with the Young Musicians Foundation under Lawrence Foster and then Michael Tilson Thomas; I got a job traveling around the world with conductor Roger Wagner; I was invited to Tanglewood and took masterclasses in France; I became the extra flutist with the Los Angeles Philharmonic under Zubin Mehta — these things inspired me to realize I could actually become a working musician.

By about 1989, I was working too much, day and night, and I had some pain down my leg. My doctor put me in physical therapy, but they had me do all the wrong exercises. I was diagnosed with a huge herniated disk. I decided I wasn't going to have surgery if I could avoid it, so I ended up staying in bed for a couple months. I couldn't play, of course, and when I finally got up again, I was so weak I could hardly do anything.

This was definitely worrying. I had no idea what my body would do for me, or whether I'd be able to play at all. But I realized I had to go just one day at a time and do only what I was able to do. I started by practicing for one minute — that was all I could handle. Very carefully, I went up to two minutes, three minutes. It was unbelievable. I had a notebook to keep track of my progress, and little by little I worked up to three hours. I took an entire year off of work.

During that time, I took a lot of Alexander Technique lessons, and that really saved me. I found out that I had been twisting my body too much, and I totally changed how I held the flute. I relaxed much more, changing both my stance and my attitude. I did some private teaching at my house, which I really looked forward to each week. Teaching kept me stimulated. It took a lot of patience and preparing to get myself back to work, but having missed playing so much for all that time, I came back with renewal and played better than I ever had.

That was more than a decade ago; since then I am back to working day and night. Even now, I keep learning, and every day brings new challenges and fresh inspiration. That year off reignited me and my love for music, and I feel very privileged to do what I do.

Flute Stories

Susan Hoeppner)))

Susan Hoeppner enjoys international renown as a flute virtuoso. She has performed as a guest soloist with orchestras around the world and is also in great demand as a solo recitalist. She has made numerous recordings for EMI Classics, Grammophon AB BIS, JVC Victor, Marquis Classica and King Records. Hoeppner serves on the music faculty at the University of Toronto. For more information, visit www.colwellarts.com.

My years at Juilliard were one of the best times of my life. The 18 months after I graduated, however, were really, really difficult.

I grew up in western Canada, but I knew I couldn't move back to Calgary for the kind of career that I wanted — there was much more opportunity for a soloist in a larger community. So when I graduated in 1985, I moved to Toronto and had to establish myself in a new community.

I let people know I was in the city, but things just weren't happening. I had typing skills, so I did a lot of temp work — temporary secretarial positions. I actually got called to play a few weddings and receptions, but

I turned them down. I was adamant with myself that I was not going to do background music. I was still young and cocky; if I was going to play, I was going to have people sit and listen. I felt that if I charged whatever one charges for a wedding, how could I be taken seriously as a soloist and expect to charge soloist fees?

So instead I chose temp work. I felt like I was living a double life, because I would get off work and then come home to do my real work. Those were long days, and for very little money. I remember sometimes I had only pennies to rub together. It was really hard, but I had a strong sense of my direction and what I wanted to do.

Then I was asked to play an event with the Toronto Symphony. I did a bit of networking and got to know the people. The symphony's flute section has been so incredibly supportive of me over the years. All four flutists are now my dear friends. The principal flutist, Nora Shulman, made the opportunity available for me to do a recording for the Toronto Symphony, and that was the turning point for me. I did a tour with them and the flute section began coming to my solo recitals. I made more and more contacts, and soon the concerts started coming in.

I had a lot of faith in what I did. I knew that I had something, and that it was just a matter of an opportunity for it to happen. And it did. When students ask me now about a starting solo career, I don't say, "Yes, go for it," or, "No, don't go for it." I say, "You have to want it 150-percent, because it truly is so hard." The times that you're not successful, you feel really down. You have to want it badly enough to push through all of that and reach the end of the rainbow.

Trudy Kane)))

Trudy Kane has served as principal flutist of the Metropolitan Opera for 27 seasons, and has given recitals, masterclasses, and performed with orchestras and chamber groups throughout the country. She has released a solo CD, "In the French Style," with pianist George Darden. The recording includes her transcription of the Faure violin sonata, which has also been published by Little Piper. Kane's other publications include cadenzas for the Mozart D Major Concerto, and three transcriptions for flute quartet.

Over the course of my career, I've experienced both great fortune and great loss.

I couldn't have asked for a better way to get started. After graduating from Juilliard, I lost the audition for second flute at the New York Philharmonic, but I made such a good impression that they put me on top of the sub list. The first time I subbed, it was the most exciting thing I could imagine. Pierre Boulez was the music director, and just sitting there listening to those people play was wonderful. Realizing I was a part of it was even better.

My timing was perfect because there was a great deal of illness in the section, and for the next two years I was subbing with the Philharmonic for fifty percent of its performances. That meant subbing in every chair, including principal. It also meant a lot of sight-reading.

That got around town very quickly, and I became very busy freelancing. The phone was ringing all the time. I was always busy doing the best work, and I was surrounded by the best musicians. Toward the end of the second year I began subbing at the Metropolitan Opera. Shortly after that, there was an opening and I was hired. It was an exciting period in my life.

To take a very different tone, I recently went through a difficult time when my husband Harvey Estrin passed away. Before that, I didn't work for more than six months. I was taking care of him, and the flute had to be put aside. There was no other way to do it. I thought it was rough going through the experience with my husband, but the aftermath is at least as hard emotionally, if not harder.

Returning to work and playing after those months away has helped me feel more like myself again. The act of playing reinforces who I am; it gives me a much stronger sense of myself than I might feel if I didn't have the flute in my life.

Flute Stories

Mindy Kaufman)))

Mindy Kaufman has played with the New York Philharmonic since 1979. She has been piccolo and assistant principal flute with the Rochester Philharmonic and has played with the Boston Symphony Orchestra and the Milwaukee Symphony. Kaufman has performed on numerous film soundtracks and has recorded songs on albums by Madonna and Diana Krall. She serves on the faculty of The Juilliard School. For more information, visit www.newyorkphilharmonic.org.

The first audition I ever took was for second flute of the Rochester Philharmonic. I tried out just to see what it would be like to take an audition. I was 19, going into my junior year at Eastman, and a lot of the people auditioning were other Eastman students who were older than me. I practiced as if I was going to win, but I wasn't nervous because I had no expectation of winning.

We played the first round behind a screen, and then they called out the names of the people who would play another round ... and I was one of them. I was thrilled to be chosen. Some of the people I was up against were stars of the school, so making the first cut was enough for me. I played really well again in the next round — I just did my own thing and didn't worry about winning a job. And when the round was over, I had won. They decided to hire me.

I was on air. I was on cloud nine. It was so exciting, because I felt a lot of pressure from my family at that time over what I was going to do for a living. A lot of parents don't want their kids to go into music, because it's so hard to find work. Now the pressure was off — I had a job. It wasn't full-time, but I'd be making about $20,000 a year, which was great back in 1976. And my teacher was the first flutist, so that was also exciting.

My second audition didn't go quite so smoothly. It was also with the Rochester Philharmonic, for a better position in the orchestra, and I was really nervous this time because I wanted the job. I failed to advance past the first round.

An hour later, I was sitting in this restaurant called Mugs Up across from the school, having a beer or two with a friend. Someone from the audition came in looking for me and said, "Mindy, you're in the finals. They added more people, and you're one of them." I went immediately from, "Oh poor me, I didn't get the job," to drinking coffee and trying to sober up so I could go back and play. I suddenly felt this determination — now that I was past the first round, I had it in my mind that I was going to win the job. And then I went back and won it.

I definitely don't recommend having a beer before an audition. In both cases, the reason I won was because I was prepared. I'd worked hard and knew everything backwards and forwards — not only my part, but everyone else's parts as well.

That's how you win auditions. There's luck involved too, but nobody gets lucky when they're not prepared.

Flute Stories

Katherine Kemler)))

Katherine Kemler is professor of flute at Louisiana State University, flutist with the Timm Wind Quintet, and a regular visiting teacher at the Oxford Flute Summer School in England. She has recorded on Centaur Records, as well as the Orion and Opus One labels. For more information, check out www.katherinekemler.com.

Five years ago I was diagnosed with tongue cancer. This is a horrible thing to have happen to anybody, but for a flutist it's particularly scary.

My condition was serious, and I had to undergo surgery twice to have part of my tongue removed. I didn't know whether I'd ever be able to play again — or if I could, whether it would be at the same level.

I looked for other flutists who had undergone tongue surgery, and the few that I found were very supportive. One woman gave me a lot of advice on ways of easing the pain, and what I could and couldn't eat. I also called Clem Barone, who played for many years with the Detroit

Symphony. Although he had his beaten cancer many years earlier, he was willing to talk with me about it. "Where there's a will there's a way," he told me. With this support from Clem and others, I made it through.

At that time I read a book called "Love, Medicine, and Miracles" by Bernie Siegel, which advised that if you have cancer and you want it to go away, start living your life as if you have only one year left to live. When I read the book, I thought I was already living like that, but when I sat down and thought about it, I realized that wasn't actually true.

So I made some changes in my life. I had been dating a composer for 11 years, 10 of which were long-distance since he was in Illinois. I proposed to him and he moved here to Louisiana. We're married now and really, really happy.

Looking back, the whole experience with cancer was a great blessing. It changed my outlook on life and actually improved my relationships with other flute players. Before this I had been very competitive, and I actually felt so intimidated by other great flutists that I got extremely nervous before performing. My ordeal made me realize that I play the flute because I love it and because I want to share it with other people, and therefore it doesn't matter if every performance is perfect, or if it's as good as someone else's. Because what I have to offer may not be the same as what they have. I can really appreciate other flutists and rejoice in their playing.

I won't say I never get nervous now, but I don't feel like it's a matter of life and death anymore. When I go out on stage I'm so happy to be there that it doesn't matter.

Flute Stories

Jeffrey Khaner)))

Jeffrey Khaner has been principal flute for the Philadelphia Orchestra since 1990. Previously, he served as principal flute for the Cleveland Orchestra, the Mostly Mozart Festival in New York, and the Atlantic Symphony in Halifax, Nova Scotia, and co-principal flute of the Pittsburgh Symphony. He serves on the faculty of the Curtis Institute of Music in Philadelphia and has taught and performed as a soloist throughout the world. For more information, visit www.iflute.com.

I was in the fairly unusual situation of being hired extremely young by one of the best orchestras in the world. I was thrust into a position where all of the people around me knew everything so well and did everything so well. And here I was, at 23, never having done most of these things at all.

On the one hand, it's a wonderful luxury to play a Beethoven symphony for the first time, sitting in the middle of the Cleveland Orchestra. On the other hand, you can be awfully intimidated, and there's no room for error. Your learning curve has to be much, much steeper to fit in with all of these people who are so good.

At my very first rehearsal with the orchestra, the first piece we played was Ravel's "Daphnis and Chloe," which has a big flute solo in it— and it was also the first time I'd ever played it. The orchestra didn't even rehearse, we just ran through it. I don't really remember anything about how I felt during the performance because I too busy thinking about so many things. At the end, the conductor looked at me and said, "Is there anything you want to do over again?" I believe I must have quivered while saying, "No." The rest of the orchestra laughed, because they knew it was the first piece I'd ever played with them, and that was it — we went on to the next piece.

But several years later, the piccolo player at the time, Bill Hebert, told me that after having heard the first scale in my solo, he knew I had it under control and that things would work out for me.

It wasn't the last time I found myself in that position. Many of the pieces we performed — even by composers like Beethoven and Brahms — I had never played before, because you only get a limited amount of experience in school. It's a part of growing up, along with the realization that the way one plays in a professional situation is totally different than the way one plays as a student. I felt a tremendous sense of responsibility as a professional that I had never felt in school.

Over the 20-odd years that I've been playing in orchestras, my main inspiration has come from the people who are sitting around me. Every once in a while I've had a conductor provide inspiration, but more often it comes from the people in the orchestra. Hearing the way my colleagues play, and just trying to match the standards that they set, has always helped make me a better player — then and now.

Flute Stories

Stephen Kujala)))

Stephen Kujala is principal piccoloist with the Hollywood Bowl Orchestra. He has toured and collaborated with jazz pianist Chick Corea and was featured ethnic flutist for the musical "The Lion King" in Los Angeles. He can be heard on several hundred movie soundtracks, TV shows, commercials, and records, including his own debut recording "Fresh Flute."

When I was in eighth grade I was the only male flutist in an 18-girl flute section of the school band. As you can imagine, my guy friends made fun of me for playing what was considered to be a sissy instrument.

That's a very sensitive age because you're under a tremendous amount of peer pressure to conform to what everybody else is doing — wearing the same clothes, doing the same things, playing a cool instrument. I ended up buckling under the pressure. After the eighth grade, I decided: "No more. I'm quitting."

This was the summer of 1969, when everybody was wearing their hair long and the Beatles were in full bloom. I got more and more into rock and roll, and I spent the summer before high school playing electric guitar, growing my hair long, smoking cigarettes, and doing whatever else I had to do to be considered cool. I dropped the flute altogether.

This was much to the chagrin of both my parents. My father is a flutist, and he was really grooming me to become an orchestral flutist and follow in his footsteps. But they didn't push me at all. They decided to just lay low and see what would happen when I got into high school.

On my first day of ninth grade, the high school orchestra director, Sam Mages, and the jazz band director, Roger Mills, both came to my homeroom. They asked my teacher which student was Steve Kujala, then walked over to my desk and drafted me right there and then. They said, "We hear you're a hotshot flutist, we really need you," and they did not let me say no. I reluctantly played along, and within a week I found myself playing in the jazz band, the wind ensemble, and the orchestra.

I met a guy named Steve Eisen, who was two years older than me. He played principal flute in the orchestra, principal oboe in the symphonic wind ensemble, and lead tenor saxophone in the jazz ensemble. On top of that, he played electric guitar, blues harmonica, and he smoked Old Gold filters. Everybody thought he was the coolest.

So here I had somebody I could look up to. I figured, if he could do all this stuff and be cool, I guess I could, too. Also, at that time, the rock group Jethro Tull had just come on the scene. Their frontman Ian Anderson played flute and guitar, and they were the hottest group on the planet.

So within three months I had gone from being kind of a geek to something of a local hero. I was playing in classical and jazz ensembles as well as flute and guitar in a rock band. I was having the time of my life.

Later I found out the whole homeroom incident had been engineered by my parents. Turns out Sam Mages lived just down the block from us, and they had all conspired together to get me playing flute again. If it had not been for those two teachers recruiting me, for Ian Anderson coming onto the scene, and for Steve Eisen being a cool guy, I would not be doing what I'm doing now. I have those three people and my parents to thank for my career.

Walfrid Kujala)))

Walfrid Kujala has received the National Flute Association Lifetime Achievement Award. He is a professor at Northwestern University in Chicago and played with the Chicago Symphony for almost 50 years. He and his wife, Sherry, are publishers of his books, "The Flutist's Progress" and "The Flutist's Vade Mecum." For more information, check out www.personal.utulsa.edu/~leonard-garrison/kujala.html.

I started flute lessons in 1937, during the severe economic hardship of the Depression. Unemployment was around 25 percent in this country.

At that time, my father was an amateur bassoonist. He got his first job in music thanks to funding from the Works Progress Administration — one of the many alphabet organizations that Franklin Roosevelt started as he took over the presidency in 1932. The WPA supported orchestras all over the country by subsidizing the employment of musicians like my father, who were out of work.

As I advanced and got good enough, I was invited to be a nonpaid member of the Huntington Symphony Orchestra in West Virginia, which was subsidized by the WPA. By the time I graduated from high school I had played in this orchestra for almost four years and covered an enormous amount of symphonic repertoire, which made a big difference in my level of preparation when I was accepted to the Eastman School of Music.

That was an extremely influential and inspiring period for me despite the fact that it came about as a result of the economic depression. As soon as World War II started, the WPA was phased out. My father was temporarily unemployed again, and he had to take a job as a machinist.

Public funding for the arts has suffered a decline in recent years, and the National Endowment for the Arts has been quite controversial. Many people have forgotten we have a history of government support for the arts through the WPA.

That funding was an extremely important incentive for me to actually consider becoming a professional musician. The WPA was intended as only a temporary answer to the Depression, nevertheless it showed that government support for the arts is an important thing for the morale as well as for the economic security of artists.

Robert Langevin)))

Robert Langevin is principal flute for the New York Philharmonic. He was formerly principal flute for the Pittsburgh Symphony and assistant principal for the Montreal Symphony. He has performed with Quebec's most distinguished ensembles and has recorded extensively for the Canadian Broadcasting Corporation. Langevin serves on the faculties of The Juilliard School, The Manhattan School of Music, and the Orford International Summer Festival. For more information, visit www.newyorkphilharmonic.org

It was something of an accident that I came to play the flute. I'd been playing other instruments, but I picked up the flute because in my hometown no one else was playing it. I was under the impression that it was a rare instrument.

For the first few months I had to teach myself, using method books, because I didn't know any other flute players. Although I ended up taking lessons with an amateur flutist who came to town, I didn't hear any flute recordings for maybe the first two years that I was learning the instrument.

Of course, later on I realized the flute is very popular. When I went to study at the conservatory in Montreal, there were 18 flute students in my class. I found it was not such a rare instrument after all. I certainly was at the bottom of the class, and that encouraged me to work hard because I realized I had a lot to learn. Hearing the better players inspired me as well.

The flute was a good choice for me in the long run. I started with trumpet and clarinet, but I believe the flute has the best literature of all the wind instruments. Of course it doesn't compare to what string players have, but I don't think I would have had any aptitude for strings. In the orchestra, opera, ballet, and solo literature, when compared to the other wind instruments, the flute parts are almost always more interesting. Flutists are the luckiest from that point of view.

Rhonda Larson)))

Virtuoso flutist Rhonda Larson is known worldwide for integrating her rich classical heritage with a popular fusion of Celtic, jazz, ethnic, and sacred music. She has performed throughout the world as soloist and with her five-piece band "Ventus." Larson is a Grammy Award-winning flutist and a former member of the Paul Winter Consort. She recently released her second CD, "Distant Mirrors." For more information, visit www.rhondalarson.com.

As a flute soloist, I am well acquainted with the ever-present challenges of my chosen profession. Better yet, I should clarify that my profession chose me. I was born with the desire to play the flute, and it is this original love of the instrument — its sound and beauty, and the very act of playing music — that has kept me going through all the tough times.

The tough times never involve the musical or artistic side of things. Those are always positive challenges. The tough, frequently discouraging times involve the business of music, the industry side, and being a flute player makes it tenfold as difficult as it might be if I played violin or piano

— instruments which have traditionally held prominence in satisfying public demand.

In our era, the flute has truly begun to come into its own, though it requires a ton of effort to convince music industry moguls to see it in this new way. It's not easy to convince them that the public not only *will* come to hear the flute but actually *wants* to hear a flute concert. The comment I hear most often, in all its variations, is, "I had no idea the flute could do all that — my wife made me come, and now I love the flute."

People like James Galway and Julius Baker have been a constant, living encouragement. They are living proof that the flute can have a viable presence as a solo instrument. The public's respect for the flute continues to evolve in a positive direction, and there has been no greater era for flute players than today. Because of this, I am able to follow a wider vision of what the flute can be doing in the world of music, beyond (but including) the primarily classical realm. This expansive view feeds my own personal hope and persistence in pressing onwards.

Hubert Laws)))

Internationally renowned flutist Hubert Laws is one of the few classical artists who has also mastered jazz, pop, and rhythm-and-blues genres. He has performed and collaborated with many of the world's top musicians and orchestras, such as Quincy Jones, Miles Davis, and the New York Philharmonic. He has released 20 albums and received three Grammy nominations. Laws maintains his own music publishing companies, Hulaws Music and Golden Flute Music. For more information, visit www.hubertlaws.com.

I began playing the flute for one incident, and that was to play the "William Tell Overture" flute solo. This was during my last six weeks in high school — we were going to play that piece during the school's graduation commencement, but there was no flute player in the high school band. I was playing saxophone at the time.

A friend of mine had an old flute in his attic that he was supposed to get rid of, and he gave it to me. There was no instructor available to teach me how to play it, so I struggled to learn just for that particular solo. It was a challenge, and I loved the sound of the instrument. The flute felt like a natural marriage for me, so I just kept practicing.

I went on to Texas Southern University, where there was no flute instructor, so I was forced to major on the clarinet instead. My music appreciation class involved attending the school's symphony orchestra concerts, and at one of them I happened to run into Clement Barone and David Colvig, who both played with the Houston Symphony at that time. I remember I just went right up to them and asked if I could get flute lessons. They looked at each other, and Clement Barone accepted the assignment. He ended up having a profound effect on my development as a flute player.

Later, when I auditioned for the Curtis Institute in Philadelphia, Barone assured me I would have no problem getting in. But he didn't realize there was just one opening, and they were auditioning people from all over the world, including William Kincaid's students. Before I had even returned home after the audition, there was a letter of rejection waiting for me.

That was a difficult period. After lying across the bed for awhile, depressed over my rejection, I happened to see an ad in the Local 47 union monthly publication about auditions being held for a scholarship. I entered the competition, and that's what yielded my scholarship to the Juilliard School, my opportunity to study under Julius Baker, and the beginning of my career as a flute player.

Herbie Mann)))

Herbie Mann, credited as one of the seminal jazz flutists, is also celebrated internationally for his explorations of rhythms and harmonies around the world, which began long before the concept "world music" was coined. "Balkan Caravan," his new album with his group, the Carpathian Basin Street Band, is due for release in 2003. For more information, visit www.herbiemannmusic.com.

When I started playing jazz on flute, there were no other flutists who only played jazz. All the guys who played were doublers. So I got flak from other jazz musicians, because there was nothing they could identify with — there was no jazz history for flute, period.

Kenny Clark was a great drummer. He said to me, "I don't think the flute is a jazz instrument." I said, "I don't think any instrument is any genre. It's just an instrument, until whoever plays it decides what he wants to do. If you want to play the polka and play a sousaphone, then you're a polka sousaphone player."

When I started playing straight-ahead jazz, no one could comprehend what this instrument was doing playing this music. The minute I added Latin percussion, all of a sudden it became logical to the public, because in other cultures the flute has always been a soloist instrument. That helped people to understand what this was.

About six years ago, I was diagnosed with inoperable prostate cancer. When that happened, I realized it was possible that my next record would be my last record. At this point in my life I had played all kinds of genres from all over the world, but I wasn't Brazilian, I wasn't Jamaican, I wasn't Japanese — what I am is I'm a second-generation European Jew. I had tried for years to stay away from that music, because there was already a klezmer movement, but I finally decided to go beyond klezmer and really look into the whole picture.

My music now is "Carpathian Basin," for want of a better genre, because it incorporates music from that entire region — Gypsy, Croatian, Bulgarian, Hebrew, everything. I've just come back from Hungary, where I finished an album with Hungarian musicians. Like playing the flute in jazz when nobody understood that, I'm pushing the envelope again.

The flute has been used as a solo instrument by cultures all over the world, but in America this role is still very new. And I feel that if this is my last record, my legacy is set.

Göran Marcusson)))

Göran Marcusson has played with the Gothenburg Opera, Finnish Radio Symphony Orchestra, and London Symphony Orchestra, and currently plays with the GöteborgsMusiken Chamber Ensemble in Sweden. For many years, he has been among the family of artists at the Newport Music Festival. He performs and teaches masterclasses around the world. For more information, visit www.fluteconnection.net/contfl/contfl.html.

My general "problem" was that I started playing flute relatively late. I was a fluteowner from age 8, but did not care at all until I was 14 or 15. My teacher at that time encouraged me to try for the conservatory in Stockholm. I was not accepted.

I thought with a year of practice I'd get to where I should be. So, a year later I auditioned again, and this time also to conservatories in Göteborg and Malmö, just to be sure I'd have a place. Again, I was not accepted.

That was hard. I started to realize that I wasn't going to be a musician. I had no talent. At age 19, I was thinking, "Now what?" I decided to do one final round of auditions before attending university. I was not accepted.

But, this time I made it to the final rounds at two colleges. I decided to read music history at the university and practice like never before. I thought understanding music history might be a bonus at my auditions. I took a few private lessons and became very well prepared. Eventually I tried again, and was not accepted. Not even close. At none of the conservatories.

Who was I? Was I wasting my life? At 20 years old, I had no other interests — music was my life! I loved the opera, the ballet, Puccini, Berg, Verdi, Prokofiev. I spent so much time in the orchestra halls, not to mention the Royal Opera House. I saw "Romeo and Juliet" seven times, and one season I saw 14 out of 16 performances of "La Bohème." I played along with discs at home: Beethoven, Rimsky-Korsakov, the Chicago, Boston, and London orchestras.

However, I did get a job with a local tram company in Göteborg, driving trams or busses three days a week and playing in their wind band. I took private lessons and lived for my flute. I just never stopped practicing. Finally, at 21, I was ready for another audition round. And ... I was not accepted.

Okay, well at least I now had a life I kind of liked. Maybe I didn't need the conservatory? Some people insisted I could make it without school, like lots of jazz players. But I still had dreams of playing with the great orchestras, and I knew I had things to learn. So, I went for my first masterclass ever when I was 23. It was with William Bennett, and it was a shock — I learned so much! Partly, I learned why I'd never been accepted at the auditions, and I learned how to please the judges. But also, I realized how much I actually already knew about flute playing compared to many of my friends who did go to conservatories.

Both Wibb and Trevor Wye opened doors to my life of music. After studying with them, I decided to try a final audition at the Conservatory in Göteborg. Why again? I realized I would need contacts to get into the local music scene. Also, maybe this was stupid, but I wanted free lessons and to play more with strings and ensembles, not just winds. This time I made number 2 on the waiting list. (The guy before me on the list is today principal at the Royal Stockholm Philharmonic.)

Then, on my 24th birthday, I finally got the letter I had waited for so long. I was accepted.

The thing I never lost during the hard times was my love for the music. Discovering Mahler and Shostakovich symphonies, great operas, Honegger symphonies, and so much more. The love and joy I experienced from the music was so strong, and I think that was what kept me going — I just knew I had to do things like that in the future. And I sure did.

Flute Stories

Robin McKee)))

Robin McKee is associate principal flute with the San Francisco Symphony. Previously, she played with the Baltimore Symphony and performed with both the Oklahoma All-State Orchestra and All-State Band during her high school years. For more information, visit www.sfsymphony.org.

At the end of my sophomore year at Oberlin, my teacher Robert Willoughby made two fellow students and I learn excerpts for our juries. This was something sophomores usually didn't have to do. He had us playing Strauss's "Till Eulenspiegels" and Prokofiev's "Classical Symphony" — pieces which were a little beyond me.

I was so frustrated, I started crying during the lesson. Then Willoughby gave me the only pep talk I ever needed: "You may win your first audition or you may win your hundredth audition, but keep working at it and you'll get it right."

I had a hundred times to get it right if I needed it. I always remembered that.

Susan Milan)))

Susan Milan was the first woman to be appointed principal of the Royal Philharmonic Orchestra, sparking a multi-dimensional career as orchestral principal, chamber musician, teacher, and international soloist. She is a prolific recording artist, has performed numerous world premieres, and has inspired many contemporary composers to write for her. In addition to duo partnerships, she has formed the London Sonata Group, London Debussy Trio, and Instrumental Quintet of London. For more information, visit www.master-classics.com.

The frog living in the well looks up at the bright circle of sky and thinks, "I am king. I see and understand all."

I was 19 and in my third year at the Royal College of Music when I traveled to Boswil, Switzerland for my first masterclass with Marcel Moyse. I had been studying with John Francis, who was a marvelous teacher and mentor, but his praise and kindness had overwhelmed me and I had fallen into a comfortable well.

As soon as I had a chance, I confidently jumped up to play for Moyse. I thought I would really impress this famous French teacher! The platform was bursting with well-known international flute players, although I did not know them, because I had been a "frog in a well" for so long. And so I gave my rendition of "Pan" from Roussel's Joueurs de flûte. Silence. Silence for what seemed a lifetime. Then the great maestro said very loudly, "You tongue like a duck."

Nobody spoke, and my confidence was shattered. My entire world closed in on me and my legs were reduced to jelly. He was right. I had not been taught to tongue in the light "French" style, but how was I to know? After a grueling lesson in front of players such as James Galway, Michel Debost and William Bennett, Moyse saw me after class for a private lesson on articulation which was magical. I clearly needed a new approach.

Anyway, I was a plucky young thing so I decided I would again play for Moyse during this course, but this time something which showed off my finger technique. And so I played Andersen's study, opus 15 no. 3, rather fast. I thought, "I may not have got the hang of the tonguing yet, but I shall show them I can move my fingers!" Was I nervous! But up I got and rattled through it. Moyse simply said, "Why you play so fast?"

After three weeks I went home humbled, inspired, and armed with many notes. I still studied with John Francis and worked with my notes on Moyse's interpretations. The next year in Boswil, I played Ibert's Piece for Flute. Moyse seemed happier with my playing and that Christmas sent me a card reading:

> "Meilleurs voeux- sante- success
>
> I remember very well — piece par Jacques Ibert
>
> Et brillant scale in 3rds
>
> Do not be so nervos, Best souvenirs, Marcel Moyse"

For my post-graduate year, I studied with Geoffrey Gilbert, working only on studies, scales and exercises. It was a joy with such a remarkable teacher. The following year I played the Suite by Benjamin Godard for Moyse. He said, with his bright blue eyes twinkling, "What has happened? You are the real artiste." This was a dream come true — a compliment to treasure.

After I joined the Royal Philharmonic Orchestra, I still visited the Moyse courses. His voice with its rich French timbre, his directness and kindness, are unforgettable. I still see him dancing to Doppler's "Hungarian Pastoral Fantasie" and praying in Gounod's "Ave Maria," and I never once play the Godard Suite without seeing his face and hearing his voice.

The moral of this story? There is a big world outside the well. Jump, look and listen, before it is too late.

Matt Molloy)))

Matt Molloy is widely recognized as the master of Irish traditional flute playing. He has been a member of the Chieftains since 1979 and has released four acclaimed solo albums. In 2000, Molloy was awarded the first-ever prestigious National Traditional Musician Award by TG4, the Irish-language TV station. In addition to playing, Molloy owns a pub in Westport, Ireland, called Matt Molloy's, well-known for hosting traditional live music. For more information, visit www.mattmolloys.com or www.thechieftains.com.

Traditional Irish flute playing is an aural tradition. I come from the west of Ireland, a place called Ballaghadereen, and there was a musical background in my family, particularly my father's side. It was never a profession — it was just a hobby, just part of who you were. When my father saw I was interested, he started teaching me reels and jigs on an old, "simple system" open-holed flute.

I played in school, and over the years I won a number of competitions, including the All-Ireland Championship, which was good encouragement. Then, when I was about 18, I went to Dublin and started to play in folk clubs with musicians I met there. But I never considered music as a professional career. At that time in Ireland, everyone wanted to hear ballads; there was no real interest and very little outlet for instrumental music.

So I went to school for four years to take the aircraft engineering exams. Then I went to work for Aer Lingus, the national airline, and I was with them for about 11 years.

In the '60s there was a general upsurge in folk music, and a lot of the clubs, lounges, and hotels running ballad nights around Dublin started to introduce some traditional instrumental music into these shows. For us, that was an opportunity to make a little spending money. I got together with a group of fellows and one girl and we started a band called the Bothy Band. I got leave of absence from Aer Lingus for six months. Then I got another leave of absence for a further six months. When I applied for a third, they said, "No no, Matt, it's time to make up your mind." So I did.

After leaving my job, I woke up at night with panic attacks every now and again, saying, "Jesus, what did I do?" I'd just got married and had a house mortgage and one kid at the time, and our money dropped by half. The Bothy Band's music has held up surprisingly well and has influenced a lot of young musicians since then, but from a financial point of view it was a disaster. The music was the easy part — keeping a proper discipline on ourselves, we weren't very good at. There was a lot of drinking at the time, and eventually things sort of fell apart.

While I was with the Bothy Band, I noticed my health wasn't as good as it should be. I had trouble with breathing, and I went to the local GP. He gave me something for a chest infection and said it was just bronchitis, not to worry about it, but after awhile it still hadn't cleared. So I went back and asked for an X ray. He said, "You're imagining things." But we got the X ray, and it transpired that I had tuberculosis.

That scared me. I really thought the game was up, that it was all over — that it meant going back to some sort of day job. But I spent two months healing up in a TB ward, and that was a wake-up call. I came in off the fast lane and had time to think and reflect. I discovered I had no insurance, which was a big shock, and I realized how selfish I'd been. I had a family and a kid, and I had no insurance. That was stupidity.

The spell in hospital and the recovery period motivated me. I vowed then that things had to change — I couldn't carry on like this. I started working harder and playing more — on my own, in duets and trios, and things like that. The Bothy Band wasn't going anywhere, so we decided to give it a rest, and soon after I was hired by a popular band at the time called Planxty. We recorded an album and toured it for almost a year, and when that project was over, I got word that the Chieftains were interested in taking me on. So that's when I joined the Chieftains, and I'm still here. Financially things improved a lot.

Committing myself to music was the best thing I ever did, but at the time I didn't think so, and a lot of people around me didn't think so either. I had a career and an education, and as skilled trades go, working on aircraft was a good one. But now I'm doing what I really want to do, and that makes all the difference.

Ervin Monroe)))

Ervin Monroe is principal flute for the Detroit Symphony Orchestra. He has performed with the Mozarteum Orchestra, the Chamber Symphony of Philadelphia, and the Royal and Bolshoi ballets, and in duo-concerts with such renowned artists as the late Jean-Pierre Rampal. Monroe is an active recording artist and has published numerous original compositions and arrangements. For more information, visit www.muramatsu-america.com.

In 1965, I was in New York looking for a job. I was working on my master's degree at the Manhattan School of Music, and my wife was pregnant. She'd been working as a model, but as she got more and more pregnant she had to give that up. We'd run out of money, and I had to make a decision.

I knew it was going to be hard suddenly having another mouth to feed, and I was really on the verge of giving up my dream of playing in an orchestra. I was trying to figure out whether I should get a part-time job at a music store, find a fellowship somewhere, or go for a doctorate and get a college job.

The Manhattan School office told me they'd had a call from a parks band up in Connecticut that needed a flutist for the summer. It didn't pay very much, but to supplement the income they arranged, as part of the job, for me to drive a milk truck in the morning for the local dairy. I'd be getting up at 5 every morning to make deliveries for three or four hours. It was so the milk drivers could take a vacation.

My wife was going to deliver at any moment, and I was pretty serious about taking the job. I told them to give me a week to think about it.

I got another call from a friend, a flute player from New York, who had to cancel out on a job the next day in New Jersey. It was just a one-day job with a local pickup orchestra, but I went and played, and the principal bassoon player on that job asked me if I was interested in doing a ballet tour. I said, "Well, yeah. I'm wondering what I'm going to do for next month's rent." He told me there was an opening for the Royal Ballet because somebody had canceled, and gave me a number to call.

I auditioned the next day, and the contractor told me, "We don't know you or anything about you, but we're going to sign a contract with you that says if it doesn't work out, you'll agree to move down to second flute." It was unbelievable. Suddenly I had one of the top touring jobs in New York.

The next day my wife gave birth to a set of twins. We had a one-bedroom apartment with a fold-out bed, and of course two kids was one more than we had expected. There was no way of scanning back then to find out what you were going to have. So I ended up sleeping in the bathtub until we finally got a crib.

I started a week later with the Royal Ballet at the old Metropolitan Opera, and after the first week they tore up my contract and gave me a raise. It was a turning point for me — not only was the job was very lucrative, but it also opened up a lot of doors for me and got my name around. I ended up playing with the Bolshoi Ballet and Danish Ballet and several others, just from that one connection. And it was great preparation for playing at the next level.

    The whole thing was like a fairy tale come true.

Flute Stories

Claude Monteux)))

Claude Monteux has established a dual international career as both concert flutist and conductor, and has recorded extensively. He served as Music Director of the Columbus Symphony and the Hudson Valley Philharmonic, and has served on the faculties of the New England Conservatory of Music, the Peabody Conservatory, Vassar College, Ohio State University, and San Diego State University. He is musical advisor of the Pierre Monteux School in Hancock, Maine. Monteux may be contacted at c77ux@earthlink.net.

Twenty years ago I became unable to play the flute because of a neurological movement disorder called dystonia. I was 62, and I was still growing in terms of facility and understanding of music, so for me, it was the greatest tragedy.

I was on the faculty of the New England Conservatory at the time, and I was due to play a summer concert in Maine with a very fine group called the Composers Quartet. I was practicing the Prokofiev Sonata for Flute and Piano. After 60 years of playing I was used to hearing certain results from my flute, but this time the notes would not play the way I wanted them to. I had a student in my studio, and I said, "Can you see anything wrong with the way I'm holding my flute?" She said, "Your lower lip is sticking way up."

It took at least eight months before somebody found out what it was. I went to different doctors, including acupuncturists and everything under the sun, until someone suggested a neurologist. I found one who immediately diagnosed it, and she referred me to a doctor who had a treatment called botulinum toxin — now known as botox. The treatment, which I'm still taking, calls for a large set of injections in the face and around the eyes. The injections have to be repeated every three months.

Before this I had divided my life between conducting and playing, but I don't find conducting very satisfying. I've always preferred to play. As a performer, I have one high point which I look back on and cherish: My father was the famous conductor Pierre Monteux. In 1963, he and I recorded together for London/Decca. It was a very good record and sold well, and because I made it with my father I would say that was the high point of my life.

Having to give up the flute meant having to give up the only way that I could really express myself musically. But dystonia hasn't kept me from teaching. I have between seven and 10 students, and they're all very gifted. I play the piano just well enough to accompany them.

There are times when life doesn't seem so much fun, especially when I'm in pain. But I can enjoy waking up in the morning because I still love teaching, and I look forward to seeing my students. I believe that my purpose in life is to transmit my knowledge to my them. I feel very lucky that I'm able to do that.

Flute Stories

Alexander Murray)))

Alexander Murray is professor of flute at the University of Illinois at Urbana-Champaign, as well as director of the Urbana Center for the Alexander Technique. He is former principal flute for the London Symphony Orchestra, served on the faculty of the Royal Dutch Conservatory, and taught at the Interlochen National Music Camp in Michigan for 32 years.

The flute came naturally to me at first. I played in a university orchestra when I was 13, and my first teacher, David Sanderman, once told my wife that he thought teaching was no problem at all. That was when I was his only student. Another teacher of mine was Robert Murchie, a nice old man who drank rather heavily, and his method of teaching was just patting you on the back and saying, "That's very nice, laddie, see you next time."

Then I went into the Air Force, in 1947, at which point I started lessons with a teacher in London. I won't mention his name, but within two lessons he had me reduced to not being able to play a note.

This teacher told me everything I did was wrong. He wanted me to keep a forced smile on my face and move my jaw backwards and forwards. He demanded a totally different way of playing than the way in which I was used to. When I asked him why I had to do these things, he said, "If you want to have lessons with me, you have to do as I say." Which is a very poor reason for doing anything.

I stuck at it, but it was totally destructive. I couldn't play. I had a sort of nervous breakdown, so the Air Force gave me 10 days off. I won't blame my breakdown entirely on this teacher — he just happened to be the catalyst — but after six lessons I was posted in the Far East, which was the best thing that could have happened to me. I had to start over and sort things out for myself. It took me two years to do that.

I don't believe a teacher should ever be discouraging, and the way he imposed his method on me was not at all what I needed. However, I'm grateful for that teacher because he made me rethink my playing, instead of just going on in the way that I'd played naturally, which had certain limits. There comes a time in everyone's life when you have to think for yourself and find your own way, and the earlier it happens, the better.

Flute Stories

Emmanuel Pahud)))

Emmanuel Pahud has returned as principal flutist of the Berlin Philharmonic Orchestra, a position he previously held from 1993 to 2000. He has also served as principal flute of the Munich Philharmonic and Basel Radio Symphony orchestras, and has taught at the Conservatoire de Genève. He performs as an award-winning recitalist, chamber musician, and with top orchestras throughout the world. Pahud now records exclusively for EMI Classics International. For more information, visit www.fluteconnection.net/contfl/pahud.html.

I had a very good life for 30 years, with no real problem apart from the normal challenges of moving forward in a career. Everything was going really well until a recent period, when I went into personal troubles like separation and divorce.

I try to separate my private life from my professional life as much as possible. But being on the road makes it rather difficult to have continuous contact with home, and obviously this kind of life is not easy to share with a partner. This problem is not particular to musicians — it's true for businessmen, politicians, or for any person pursuing a successful career. The standards are high now, so if you want to be successful you have to dedicate a lot of time to your career, and this can cause problems in relationships.

There are other personal difficulties to consider. Once people see you as successful, many of them behave differently, which makes it very difficult to separate who are your friends from who are the ones who want to make use of your success. Whether in a friendship or a business relationship, it's not always easy to know the intentions of the people you are dealing with. This is something I regret a little, but it is certainly part of being successful.

Despite these problems, my flute playing itself has never suffered. The flute has always been a relief and a pleasure, never related to any pain physically or psychologically. I've always enjoyed myself onstage, and the fact that I've been busy playing the flute, learning different pieces, traveling around the world, and getting to meet new people has certainly helped me get through difficulties in my private life. I try to live my life in an intense way and enjoy time on earth, whether I'm onstage or offstage.

As musicians, it's important that we share our lives and our passions during performances. People who come to our concerts expect not only that we entertain them, as though they were in front of a TV or in a cinema — they expect more from us. Active listening means that when people buy tickets to a live show, they want us to really share some time and passion from our lives with them, not just repeat automatic gestures that we've learned.

Keeping it fresh is a matter of attitude. You can play the Mozart Concerto in G for the 200th time, and it's still going to be a different piece depending on where and with whom you're playing it. Also, you don't play the same when you're 20 as you do when you're 30 or 40. Depending on what time of your life you're playing this piece, you see it in a very different way. I've certainly played the Mozart G and D concertos over 100 times each, but I'm not yet tired of playing them. I discover new things in each performance — interesting features in the horn or string parts, for instance.

Pursuing the goal and ideal of being a musician is something that continually draws me forward and helps me through any bad periods. The flute playing and music making are a big part of my life — they have been and will be. Looking back, I could have pursued other options, but I do not regret my choices and I wouldn't want to change.

Susan Palma-Nidel)))

Susan Palma-Nidel has been a member of the Orpheus Chamber Orchestra since 1980. She is principal flute for the American Composers Orchestra and Speculum Musicae, and has performed as principal flutist and soloist with such groups as the Stuttgart and Royal Ballets and the Bach Chamber Soloists. She can be heard on more than 50 recordings for Deutsche Grammophon, Columbia, Nonesuch, NewWorld, CRI, London, and Bridge records. For more information, visit www.orpheusnyc.com.

My first year out of Juilliard, I was frustrated and depressed because I felt that something about my playing wasn't working. I had all these ideas in my head and my heart, and I wasn't able to project them. It got to the point where I thought, "I'm not enjoying this. I don't like how I sound, and I can't figure out why. Maybe I shouldn't be playing the flute."

I talked about this with a friend of mine, Erich Graf, who's played for years with the Utah Symphony, and he said, "There's this flute player named Tom Nyfenger — he's a pretty interesting guy and a really good musician. Why don't you give him a call?"

So I set up a meeting, and at my first lesson with Tom, I played a Bach sonata. I didn't feel very good about my performance, but when it was over he said, "Well, you need some accompaniment." He sat down at the piano and played the sonata from memory, and somehow just playing together was very helpful.

But then he started to teach, and I was completely blown away. It was the first time I'd ever met anyone who not only could play beautifully but could also articulate with words exactly what he meant. That was the beginning of an intense year, during which I completely changed my embouchure and my style of playing. I would get up at eight o'clock every morning and practice for hours, which was something I'd never done in my life. Now that I had a path to follow and something I could understand, it was like starting all over again.

Tom was my hero because he made it possible for me to express these things I'd never been able to express before. He had so much to offer. He could sit down and play anything on the piano, all from his head. He had analyzed what made different flute players sound different ways and could imitate them with precision. And from him, I learned how to teach.

Unfortunately, Tom Nyfenger is no longer around. He was a very tortured person, never satisfied with what he did, and he died very young. He was an unusual character but a brilliant teacher. If I hadn't met him, I don't know what would have happened to me as a flutist. He certainly made it possible for me to find my own voice. He gave me the confidence to go on, and he helped me regain my love for music and for playing.

Michael Parloff)))

Michael Parloff has been principal flutist for the Metropolitan Opera since 1977 and performs as recitalist and concerto soloist throughout North America, Europe, and Japan. He has recorded extensively, and his solo CD "The Flute Album" surveys 200 years of classic repertoire. His annotated volume, "Opera Excerpts for Flute," (Theodore Presser) was a top prizewinner in The National Flute Association's 2001 Newly-Published Music Competition. Parloff serves on the faculty of Manhattan School of Music.

I graduated from Juilliard in 1974 with only a rudimentary knowledge of audition processes and basic orchestral excerpts. I had studied with Arthur Lora, a gentleman then in his 70s, who in his heyday had played principal flute at the Metropolitan Opera and had held the first flute position in Arturo Toscanini's legendary NBC Symphony.

Surprisingly, Mr. Lora never took an audition in his life. In his day conductors were autocrats; their word was law. Toscanini would order the personnel manager to "Take that man" — in those days it was always men — "and put him in that chair," and it was done. Mr. Lora came from a world where experience, reputation, and recommendations determined the course of a career, not auditions. So he felt little sympathy for the 1970s world of union-supervised, behind-the-screen auditions. From his perspective, he was there to teach me how to play the flute; audition preparation was entirely my own responsibility.

After leaving Juilliard, I entered New York's flutist-glutted market and made my way slowly up the freelance ladder. One day as I was scanning job ads, I came across a small, enticing notice. Sandwiched between a couple of ads aimed at club-date musicians ("Comedy by Pinky!" "Funny Musicians Make More Money!"), it read: "Principal Solo Flute, Berlin Philharmonic. Send Resume to Columbia Artists Management." I wrote out my embarrassingly sparse resume — it said, basically, "Went to Juilliard" — dropped it in the corner mailbox, and forgot about it.

Several months went by. Then one afternoon when I came home and flipped on my answering machine, out rasped this thickly accented voice: "Ze audition for ze Berlin Philharmonic vill be *tomorrow* at Carnegie Hall! Be zhere at tvelve o'clock!"

In a state of near panic I called the personnel manager of the Berlin Philharmonic and asked him what exactly would be on the audition. His answer: "Ze Uzual!"

Having no idea what "Ze Uzual" meant, I showed up the following day at the stage door, clutching my copy of Mozart's D Major concerto to my chest. I was led to a small backstage room, filled with other equally ill-looking young flutists. We sat staring at each other like condemned prisoners until the personnel manager came for us. One by one each flutist was removed from the room, only to return five minutes later looking vaguely bewildered.

Finally it was my turn. I was ushered down a corridor to the main stage. Among the many things I did not know at the time about auditions was that when a German orchestra auditions an applicant, the *whole orchestra* is invited to come listen. Pinching myself, trying to wake up from this horrible nightmare, I slunk onto the stage of Carnegie Hall, having no idea what I was going to be asked to play, and found myself looking out at the entire Berlin Philharmonic. Sitting at an upright piano at the base of the stage was Herbert von Karajan.

He asked, "What did you bring to play?" I peeled the Mozart Concerto away from my chest and held it to out to him. He took the part, banged out a few introductory bars, and I launched into the opening scale. Then he snapped, "Thank you!" and I was led back to the little room filled with shell-shocked flutists.

Needless to say, I did not get the job. I did, however, receive the most valuable crash course imaginable in the current realities of orchestra auditioning. And, believe me, I never showed up unprepared for another one.

Flute Stories

Donald Peck)))

Donald Peck has received the National Flute Association Lifetime Achievement Award. He served as principal flute for the Chicago Symphony Orchestra for 42 years. Previously, he served as principal flute of the Kansas City Philharmonic and played in the Seattle Symphony. Peck has made more than orchestral 300 recordings on 12 labels. He serves on the faculty of DePaul University in Chicago. He may be contacted at dvpchi@aol.com.

I was first flute in Chicago for 42 years, and some people say, "How could you do that for so long and keep it interesting?" My answer is that I always tried to make every performance different.

Some musicians think that if they play all the notes and all the dynamics, and have a good tone, that's all there is. For me that was never the case. I've always wanted to play music, but not just notes. I want to have some feeling, some emotion there, but not just to superimpose my own. It has to be from the composer, and that requires study — reading about composers and the years they lived, and applying their styles. There are some wonderful flute players with beautiful sound and incredible technique, but after 10 minutes of a recital you're bored to tears. You've got to be ready with the notes and the dynamics, of course, but that's just the beginning of our jobs as performers. Adding music is what it's all about.

So much of that involves tone quality. When I was a student, learning the repertoire, I began to realize I was using a different sound for works by different composers. I had a smaller, brighter tone for Mozart — a clearer sound than I would use for Wagner or Richard Strauss. The same thing happened with Debussy. It wasn't on purpose at first, but I began to take note. Some people were disturbed by the fact that I switched between different sounds and styles, but I was attracted by the possibilities.

Fortunately, different conductors bring a different aura to every piece and every performance, and I've always tried to pick up on that. If I didn't like the way it went, oh well — they're gone next week and I'm still here, right? I've made five recordings of Mahler's First Symphony with the Chicago Symphony Orchestra, and you can imagine how many performances we've given over the years. We've done Brahms's Fourth Symphony 124 times. If it were the same way every time, wouldn't it be a little tiring?

Flute Stories

James Pellerite)))

After more than five decades of performing as principal flutist with the orchestras of Philadelphia, Detroit, Indianapolis, Chautauqua, N.Y., and Puerto Rico, James Pellerite made a late-life career switch to the Native American flute. In creating, performing, and promoting new music for this instrument, Pellerite's collaborations have led recently to recordings with the Polish Radio National Symphony Orchestra. For more information, contact Zalo/JP Publications at (719) 590-4896 or jpflute@aol.com.

When I was 12 and playing in the Pennsylvania All-State Band, the guest conductor planned a clinic and requested that the first-chair woodwind students each demonstrate their instruments. He was an intense conductor, and he gave us very little encouragement. The more he criticized, the worse I played, until I fell apart completely and the situation was a lost cause. I'm certain my contribution to the clinic was nil.

Afterwards, I related the story to my grandmother. She was always very attentive to my daily practice and my musical development, and though she knew nothing about music, she tried to encourage me by stressing the importance of the work ethic. She impressed upon me that anytime I failed at school or at playing the flute, "You need to pick yourself up and get on with it." Everything comes to us through hard work.

After World War II, when I enrolled in Juilliard, I faced another uphill battle. The competition was intense, and I suddenly felt that I was at the bottom of the heap. Many Juilliard students had come from the High School of Music and Art in New York, a famous school that harbored great professional talent. I was from a coal town in Pennsylvania, and I'd had no previous formal instruction. Arriving at Juilliard was not a comfortable feeling, and I felt as if someone forgot to put out the welcome mat for me.

My first semester, I didn't make any of the Juilliard orchestras, but I refused to be discouraged. While my flute teacher and dear friend Frederick Wilkins offered me encouragement, I continued to hear my grandmother's words of prior years: "Pick yourself up and get on with it." I settled in for a regimen of hard work, and I was usually among the last students to be thrown out of the practice rooms each night as they closed the building.

The next semester, I insisted on re-auditioning, and I managed to make the rotation list as an alternate. That worked out quite well for me, because by the next year I was first flute in the second orchestra. I was beginning to see the results of my labor — my musical stature was growing.

My success came not because I was extremely talented. I believed it then and I believe it now: Everything comes to us through hard work.

Flute Stories

Catherine Ransom)))

Catherine Ransom joined the Los Angeles Philharmonic as second flutist in 1996. Previously, she spent three seasons with the New World Symphony in Miami. She has been the first-prize recipient of numerous competitions, including the National Flute Association Young Artist Competition, the Flute Talk National Flute Competition, and the Chicago Flute Society Competition. For more information, visit www.laphil.org.

I graduated from Juilliard, and up until then it was as if my life had been programmed for me. I'd been through undergrad, studied for a year in England, and during my time at Juilliard I was always busy, always playing the flute. I never had to think about finding opportunities to play, or worry about making money doing it.

The hardest time for me was the year after. It was a huge shock to come out of grad school to essentially nothing. I stayed in New York, working as a T.A. in the theory department, and I played in a little regional orchestra in New Jersey, but for the most part I wasn't really playing the flute and making a living doing it. All my life I knew I wanted to play in an orchestra. I think all of us at Juilliard thought, "I'll graduate, I'll win a job, and that'll be it." For me, it took four years for that to happen.

I began taking auditions earnestly but didn't get anywhere. In three consecutive auditions that year, I never advanced past the first round. Some of them of them were pretty small orchestras as well, which was completely horrifying. At the end of that year, I couldn't see a way out. I could not imagine how I was going to make it as a flute player.

I don't want to come down too hard on Juilliard, because I think they're doing a lot better now about teaching orchestra classes, audition classes, how to make money in music, and things like that. But when I was there, grad school just didn't prepare people for the transition into the real world.

I did all sorts of things to make ends meet. I rode city buses to the East Side to teach rich people's kids in their huge houses. I played piano at a musical nursery school on the Upper East Side, improvising kids' songs. My rent was eighty percent of my income, but I managed. Winning an orchestra job was a financial concern, but more than that, it was my dream. And I couldn't see how I was going to get there.

Then a number of things happened. My teacher at Juilliard, Carol Wincenc, remained a mentor to me even after I graduated, and she really encouraged me to keep with it. The following year, I got into the New World Symphony in Miami. It was there that I learned how to audition, and I finally got the professional experience I needed. The director, Michael Tilson Thomas, is very hands-on, and not only did he give me a lot of opportunities, but it meant so much just to get encouragement from such an incredible, renowned musician.

Thanks to Carol and the whole New World experience, my luck started changing. I won a couple small auditions and then tried out for the Los Angeles Philharmonic. There were so many flute players to start with, but after four rounds it was narrowed down to two of us. Ultimately, I was chosen for the job.

It was unbelievable. I was second flute in L.A.

Alison Young Rasch)))

Alison Young Rasch has a diverse career as an orchestral principal, soloist, and teacher. She is principal flutist of the Houston Ballet Orchestra and previously held that position at the Atlanta Symphony Orchestra and the Memphis and Toledo symphonies. Featured on National Public Radio's "Performance Today," she has had works written specifically for her by several composers and has recorded on the Albany Records, Telarc and Centaur labels. For more information, visit www.alisonflute.com.

I was diagnosed with focal dystonia of the hands in March of 2001. Dystonia is a neurological disorder that causes unusual movements and cramping, which means I became unable to use my fingers in the way they were trained.

It came on slowly for about a year as I watched my skill and technique completely deteriorate. It was particularly frustrating because I was at a high point in my career: recording my second solo CD, performing in England, planning a recital tour in Brazil, serving as principal flute in an orchestra. I thought that maybe I was just out of shape and needed to practice harder.

Researchers have not been able to find a clear cause or cure for dystonia. My doctors were not unkind, but they were direct about how serious the condition is. I went through an incredible period of mourning — of loss. The question was, how could I continue to express myself musically? I didn't know if I'd have to put my flute away and never play it again.

My music director, Ermanno Florio at the Houston Ballet, watched me come unglued and said, "Hey, take a year off and figure this out. We'll hold your job for you." That was great because I was in such an emotional state that I needed someone with a level head to consider the other side of this.

I took 18 months off from performing. I saw Dr. Emil Pascarelli and his assistant Vera Wills, a musician who is highly skilled at helping affected musicians rebuild their instruments to accommodate the odd movements brought on by dystonia. She told me the choice was mine to accept my condition and then try to discover a way to make music in my limited capacity. It was very difficult for me because in the classical world we are trained that "this is the right way to do things and this is the wrong way." I had to throw all of that out the window and become creative in using all the tools that I had developed over my career to find new solutions.

I had such great support from many people — for one, I was Miss Young before I had dystonia and now I'm Mrs. Rasch! My husband, Richard Rasch, just "held my hand" through the whole nightmare. I've also been very lucky to have colleagues who have supported me — particularly Peggy Romeo, the second flutist in the Ballet's flute section.

I now play again on a somewhat limited basis, and as I improve, opportunities continue to open up for me. I take one day at a time, and I practice very carefully and deliberately. I will no longer be able to play "perfectly," but my sound, my phrasing and my understanding of music have not been affected by this condition. Some people have said they notice a deeper or more relaxed tone in my playing — maybe more of a maturity in it.

I still have something to express, and I've found that letting go of "perfection" has only enhanced the singing voice of my playing, as well as my deep desire to continue a life of music.

Flute Stories

Paul Renzi)))

Paul Renzi has served as principal flute for the San Francisco Symphony for nearly half a century. He has taught at Mills College, Stanford University, and is professor emeritus of San Francisco State University. At age 18, Renzi was named the San Francisco Symphony's principal flutist by conductor Pierre Monteux. Renzi subsequently played principal flute with the NBC Symphony under Arturo Toscanini. He returned to his present position with the San Francisco Symphony in 1957.

I recently went through quintuple bypass surgery. I was in the hospital for three weeks, but it helped that I was in good physical shape before, and within two and a half months I was working again.

I was a little worried going into surgery, but I thought, "Well, if I have to go, I'll go. That's it." The hard part was afterwards, lying in the hospital bed — at a certain point you feel like you're completely helpless. I wondered, how will I ever play the flute? You try to take a deep breath, but you can't breathe. That was a concern, because I love to work. If I'm not working, I'm bored to death.

So the worry lasted quite a while, until I got home, and after about a month I started to practice. At first it sounded god awful. But I had that goal — I kept thinking, "I've got to play, and I'm going to push myself." I looked at my schedule and planned which week I'd go back to work. When the time came around, I decided not to do it yet. I didn't want to embarrass myself. But two or three weeks later I sounded decent, so finally I called personnel and said, "I'm ready to come in."

I practice all the time because I like to play. That's the secret of success: You have to like it, and it has to be easy for you. Because if it's not easy, then it's a struggle. I'm blessed by God, it just happened. My father, Paolo Renzi, picked the flute for me because he played first oboe for the NBC Symphony, and he decided he didn't want his kid to have to shave reeds.

Actually, my first love is opera — I'm a frustrated tenor. I didn't sound too good, but I still sing as a hobby. I have all the opera scores, and I play through them on the piano. Maybe my greatest musical experience was playing flute in a series of Verdi's "Trovatori," with the San Francisco Opera in 1958 with soprano Leontyne Price. To play that opera was heaven. We would have played for nothing, it was so beautiful.

The San Francisco Symphony went on tour with Pierre Monteux in 1947. I was young and had a lot of energy, so every night after the performances I would sing. Finally, at a rehearsal, Monteux said to me, "I hear you sing tenor. You'll make a debut with me in La Bohème." And I got so scared, I thought he was serious. He was a real opera conductor.

During my career, I played Prokofiev's Fifth Symphony the first year it came out. I remember Shostakovich's Ninth and Aaron Copland's "Appalachian Spring" when they were brand new. I don't want to criticize today's music, but it's nothing like we had. It was such a great feeling to play a piece like Hindemith's "Metamorphosis" when it was new.

I just turned 77, and I realize at my age that sooner or later you have to go. But I love the flute, and I really enjoy my work. Aside from my family, playing music is the greatest thing in my life.

Paula Robison)))

Known to millions from her television appearances on "Live from Lincoln Center" and "Christmas at the Kennedy Center," Paula Robison's recordings range in repertoire from classical to Brazilian. She has given woodwind performance seminars and flute masterclasses all over the world. She has been involved with both the Italian and American Spoleto festivals as player, co-director, and noontime concert host.

The most challenging period of my life was when my husband and I were raising our daughter. Those were the years when women were being told that we could do everything all at once — we could be great artists and great mothers at the same time. Now we've begun to realize how difficult that is.

It was a joy to be with my daughter, and I loved every minute of it, and life was quite a carnival. There were times when we would be together as a family and I would think, "How can I ever practice?" Sometimes all I wanted to do was spend time with her, playing or baking cookies together.

I grew aware of how important it is to be a full-time mother. I would bring her to my rehearsals, and she would always be there drawing something while I was playing. But still it seemed impossible to balance time with her and time with my flute.

Once when she was 7 or 8, we were going to spend some family time together on Nantucket Island. Usually, I tried to get some practice time in during these family trips, but this time I said, "It's really great we have a chance to spend this time together. I don't think I'm going to bring my flute along." She replied, "But mom, I would be so sad if you weren't playing the flute." Coming from my own daughter, those words seemed so unexpected and God-sent.

During that time, there was another person who buoyed me up — a priest and dear friend named Thomas Pike. I went to him one day and said, "I just don't know how I'm going to be able to do this. Should I give up the flute for a while?" And he said, "Paula, you have to remember that your flute playing is a vocation, not just a profession. It's your art, yes, but it's a calling, too — just as much as the ministry is a calling. You're helping people every time you play that flute, and you're speaking in God's voice. Every musician is." He was stern and he was kind, and it was wonderful.

Looking back on it, it's impossible, but you have to do the impossible. Being a full-time mother is the best thing for a child, and being a musician means singing ancient songs about things that nobody really understands — songs about the eternal and the immortal. I just tried to do it all, and somehow my family and I made it through together.

Elizabeth Rowe

Elizabeth Rowe will join the National Symphony as assistant principal flute in the fall of 2003. Currently assistant principal of the Baltimore Symphony, Rowe was previously principal flute of the Fort Wayne Philharmonic and a member of the New World Symphony. She received First Prize at the 2000 National Flute Association Young Artist competition and has performed as soloist with orchestras throughout the country. She can be contacted at erowe6474@aol.com.

When I was in high school, I attended the Music Academy of the West, which is a summer music festival in Santa Barbara. I was one of the youngest people there and relatively inexperienced. Near the end of the summer I got my big shot to play principal in the orchestra, performing the "Candide" overture by Bernstein. There's a flute solo in that overture which isn't really very difficult, but rhythmically it's tricky. In the middle of rehearsal, the conductor stopped the orchestra and said to me, "First flute player, you're rushing."

We went over it again, and he stopped us again. I couldn't get it right.

We ended up going over that spot 10 or 15 times, with him stopping each time and yelling at me, getting more and more angry while I got more and more humiliated. I was fighting off tears and obviously not getting any better at it, because you can't improve too much under those circumstances.

I left the rehearsal completely horrified that in front of an orchestra of 90 people I'd made it abundantly clear that I wasn't able to do my job. But one by one, all of my colleagues — all the wind players and a lot of the brass players — came up to me afterwards and said, "Hey, Elizabeth, don't worry about it, this has happened to all of us," and "Just relax and you'll be fine. We're all behind you, and we're going to help you out."

Having all these people in my corner gave me the confidence to keep going. I went back the next day knowing they were all rooting for me, and I did okay. I don't think I was perfect, but I was much better. And by the time the concert came around, I had pretty much gotten it right.

The huge lesson I learned is that your colleagues are your best supporters — your best friends at work. A lot of challenges come and go in orchestral life, but if you maintain a good relationship with your colleagues, and treat them all respectfully and supportively, they'll return the favor. And that makes all the difference.

Gary Schocker)))

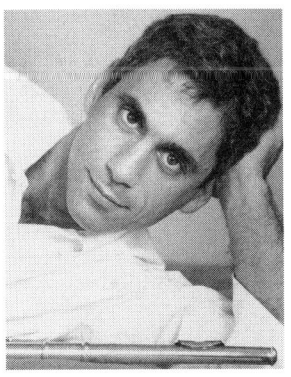

Gary Schocker has performed with such orchestras as the New York Philharmonic, the Philadelphia Orchestra, the Dallas Symphony, the West German Sinfonia, and I Solisti Italiani. In addition to his work as a flute recitalist and concerto soloist, he is a noted pianist and prolific composer, having written musicals, award-winning works for clarinet and for flute, and a wide variety of other material. For more information visit www.garyschocker.com

I won a concerto competition at music camp when I was 14, and it was suggested I go study with Murray Panitz, who was with the Philadelphia Orchestra at the time. So we scheduled a lesson, and my parents took me to see him. He listened to me play, and then said, "I really think you should consider doing something else. I don't think you've got what it takes to be a flute player."

My mom asked, "Will you teach him?"

Panitz said, "No, I really just don't have any room."

"Don't your students ever cancel?"

"No, no, they never cancel. They love me."

That was discouraging, but I always had a very strong support system. My father was my first teacher, and he let me know from day one that he thought I was terrific — and I believed him.

Then I went out for the Philadelphia Orchestra's Young People's Auditions and won. I ended up playing a concerto in front of Panitz's orchestra, which was a lot of fun for me. But he was very nice after that.

Sometimes you get a teacher who may be having a bad day, or who happens to be discouraging for whatever reason. You don't always want to take what other people say too seriously.

David Shostac)))

David Shostac, well-known for his performances throughout North America, is also a prolific recording artist and can be heard on many soundtracks of major motion pictures and television shows. He is principal flutist for the Los Angeles Chamber Orchestra, previously serving as principal flute for the St. Louis, Milwaukee, and New Orleans symphony orchestras, as well as the Mostly Mozart and Aspen Festival orchestras, among numerous other ensembles. For more information, visit www.davidshostac.com.

My parents wanted me to be a doctor. They didn't want me going into music — this unstable profession where anything could happen.

My dad was almost 60 when I was born. He was a violinist, and had been concertmaster in Dresden, Prague, Kansas City, and played for the Chicago Symphony. Then he got typhoid fever. This was before penicillin, and he developed a problem in his bowing arm. After years, he recovered, but it was one of the reasons my parents were so against me playing music for a living — you could get hurt.

My mom was a piano teacher to movie stars, and her students included

Flute Stories

the Barrymore kids. But she ended up having to get a teaching credential, and teach first grade, to support my family after my dad retired. That was another problem with a career in music — it didn't pay well.

My parents were always discouraging and then encouraging me. They gave me a quarter-size violin when I was 4. I started playing tunes, and then they took it right away again. When I was in second grade, my school band had two trombones for rent, and I raised my hand for one of them. My parents stalled until my friends got the trombones, but then they went in to talk to the teacher, and afterwards I was told I was going to play the flute. I didn't even know what a flute was at that time.

When I was in high school, I was going to be a math/science major. I had good grades, but at the same time I was going to auditions. I was also a tenor sax player for awhile, until I got banned forever from the stage at my high school because of a rock 'n' roll show that got out of hand. In fact, I almost got thrown out of school for it. But things took a turn for the good when there was a spot for a calypso flute player in a show with another student at my school — Nancy Sinatra. I guess this is how careers take shape. The tenor sax ban stayed in place, but the flute saved me!

My senior year in high school, I got into an experimental program at UCLA. I got to take science courses, but I was also able to study flute with George Drexler. My parents and I were still fighting over whether I was going to be a doctor or a musician, but meanwhile I was already playing in a band that opened for big-name rock shows and then backed up the singers. I was working with Ritchie Valens, the Johnnie Otis Show, and groups like that.

Then I was at a murder, and that really turned my parents off in regards to my musical career. I was doing a demo record with the other guys in the band — Bruce Johnson, who ended up with the Beach Boys, and Sandy Nelson, who later had a couple hits as a drummer. A record producer named John Dolphin walked into the studio. He was a big cheese at the time, and he said, "Come on boys, come down to my office and we'll talk about a deal."

When we got to his office, another guy was already there — a composer who John Dolphin had cheated on a record deal or something. They had a big argument, and Dolphin was shot. There was a fight over the gun and a knife, and I got shot in the leg.

So my mom got me out of the rock 'n' roll business. I went to Occidental College, where I was pre-med, but I continued taking flute lessons and playing on campus. I kept going back and forth on what I wanted to do. I was practicing all night and going to class in the mornings. Finally, one morning I was really tired, and during an experiment in chemistry I put the stirrer right through the bottom of the test tube, ruining the experiment. I threw it through the window and said that that was it. I decided to go into music, which was what I really wanted.

I got a scholarship to Juilliard to study with Julius Baker — a real turning point in my life. My music career had won out, and in the end, my parents finally had to accept it.

Flute Stories

Nora Shulman)))

Nora Shulman is principal flutist for the Toronto Symphony Orchestra. An active soloist, she has appeared with many orchestras, including the Detroit Symphony and the National Arts Centre Orchestra, and has been a member of the Denver Symphony Orchestra. Shulman has recorded for CBC Records and the Naxos, Centrediscs, and Marquis labels. She teaches flute at the University of Toronto and the Royal Conservatory of Music. For more information, check out www.tso.on.ca.

In 1987, at a recording session for the Toronto Symphony, I leaned over to a colleague to discuss fingerings and accidentally hyperextended the fourth finger of my left hand. There was a flash of pain. Here I was sitting on stage with microphones everywhere, ready to record, and suddenly I found myself barely able to play.

We were about to record the "Ride of the Valkyries," which is quite a technical piece, and probably one of the worst things to play with an injured left hand.

As professionals, we're trained to play, no matter what. You've got to do your job. I finished the session in considerable pain, went home, and thought a day or two of rest would put things to right. But my hand didn't get better.

I went to a doctor, but this was before sports medicine was as mainstream as it is today, and relatively few general practitioners were sensitive to the special needs of athletes and musicians. So despite the pain, I kept working. I felt it was my responsibility to do my job, although I practiced a lot less because it hurt too much to play. I made it through the season, but at the back of my mind was the fear that I had injured myself in such a way that permanently threatened my career.

When I saw things still weren't getting any better, I went to the Hamilton Musician's Clinic and saw a terrific rehabilitation specialist who concluded I had torn the fine inner muscles of my hand. He said, "The only way it's going to get better is if you stop playing, and immobilize it with a splint." So finally I put my flute down, and after about three months the muscles healed.

I learned an enormous amount from that experience — not only how to cope with scar tissue and healing muscles, but also about injury prevention. The most important thing I tell students is to always warm up very slowly. I warm up for a full half-hour before I even begin to practice, and if I'm running late for a performance I'll even warm up in the car, with my fingers on the steering wheel.

You can't take your body for granted. You have to listen not only to the music that you're playing but, just as importantly, to how your body is feeling.

Flute Stories

Renée Siebert)))

Renée Siebert has played flute for the New York Philharmonic since 1974. She has performed with the Chamber Music Society of Lincoln Center, the Barge Chamber Series, and the Orpheus Chamber Orchestra, and she teaches at the Manhattan School of Music. Siebert is active as a recording artist, and she recently released a book with Jeanne Baxtresser, "Great Flute Duos From The Orchestral Repertoire" (Theodore Presser). For more information, visit www.newyorkphilharmonic.org.

Rather than point to one inspirational moment in my career, I would have to say that my experience at the New York Philharmonic comes down to a whole series of moments — some big, some little — that are inspiring and reaffirming. And I've come to realize, over 29 years of playing there, that all these moments remind me again and again of two truths.

The first truth is the power of music, and its ability to touch people. One of those reaffirming moments came during a concert we played, a week after 9/11, of the Brahms "German Requiem." That concert helped to console people and give them hope after such a terrible tragedy. But we had performed the Requiem earlier that season, and it has a very deep effect even without following a national tragedy. I've seen that type of effect happen over and over again.

The second truth is that a person's, or an orchestra's, incredible joy and passion can make an ordinary musical experience into an extraordinary one. For me, performing Mahler's Second Symphony with Bernstein was electrifying. "Rite of Spring" with Boulez made my hair stand on end. Any of the oratorios with Kurt Masur become profound religious experiences. All of these things happen because of people's passion. And it's not just for ensembles, it's for individuals — for any of us. It's our joy that motivates us and brings us to a higher level. That's something we should never forget or take for granted. These moments don't occur every week, but when they do it's important to acknowledge them and be nurtured by them. They can help to remind you of why you wanted to become a musician in the first place and inspire you to do your best. This is what makes it happen, and this is what makes it all worthwhile.

Emily Skala)))

Emily Skala is principal flute with the Baltimore Symphony Orchestra, and she teaches at the Peabody Conservatory of Music at Johns Hopkins University in Maryland. Her debut CD, "Voices Through Time," was released in May, 2002 by Summit Records, with Grammy-winning producer Adam Abeshouse and internationally acclaimed pianist Norman Krieger. For more information about Skala, visit www.baltimoresymphony.org.

At the end of my junior year in high school, my mother announced that we were moving from Michigan to New Jersey. I wasn't really concerned about loss of friends, but I had my high school orchestra and wind ensemble and so many other activities going on. I had a wonderful musical foundation in Michigan thanks to my band director, who was so inspirational.

When we arrived in New Jersey we stopped by my new school to talk to the orchestra and band directors. They assured me they covered repertoire like Tchaikovsky and Beethoven. But when the first day of classes came around, I showed up to find there were only thirteen people in the entire orchestra, and five of them were flutists! It was quite clear there was no way we were going to play Tchaikovsky.

I was crushed. This music program was light years behind anything I had ever been a part of before. And the rest of musical life at that school consisted only of marching band, which was something I wasn't able to participate in because of a knee problem.

On top of that, I had the misfortune of displacing the school's top flute player when I arrived. She was much loved by her fellow band members, and in showing her support, it seemed her friends shied away from me. I experienced a great sense of loss that year, and for the first time I experienced the most horrible stage fright, which took many years to overcome.

Additionally, I was now commuting every other week into Queens, New York, to a new teacher who was tough and intimidating. Harold Bennett expected perfection from everybody. He had a bulldog who looked just as gruff as he did! Much of what transpired left me feeling that he had very little faith in me. His studio seemed like such a competitive and prestigious place to be, and as a teacher he was always throwing surprises at us. But I worked very diligently, and those biweekly lessons became my inspiration.

During that year I was auditioning for colleges, and I wanted very much to go to Eastman. I had a list of backup schools, too, but in the end I didn't get into any of them — that year or even the following year. It seems stage fright had gotten the better of me. I was left out in the cold.

My situation probably would have been hopeless except that Harold Bennett gave me something to grab onto: He was the first person who taught me how to practice. I will be forever grateful. During the last lesson I ever had with him, I played the Mozart Concerto in D major, and after all his skepticism and egging on, he said to me: "Now you sound like a real flutist. But don't let it go to your head."

From there I went on to study with John Krell in Philadelphia and, along with Bennett's help from the previous year, by believing in me he helped me to recover a lot of what I'd lost to stage fright. He wrote a letter of recommendation for me that was apparently so heartfelt and compelling that it caught Bonita Boyd's attention. During my third attempt to get into Eastman, she acknowledged the importance of receiving that recommendation, and how difficult it can be to make an accurate estimation of a student's playing in 15 minutes or less.

That year my dreams came true and I was accepted. The irony was that I expected to be at the bottom of the class, since all those people were being accepted when I wasn't. But it didn't turn out that way at all. I had a fruitful career there.

Many students experience a feeling of utter failure when they don't get into the school of their choice. I suffered from a great deal of self-doubt, but now I'm actually very grateful to have experienced that. Because of it I'm able to help many of my own students recover a balanced sense of self-esteem.

If you're in music at all it's because at some level you absolutely love it, hardship and all. You must remember what drew you to your art. It's very important not to lose sight of your dreams. Fulfillment lies in following your heart.

Christina Smith)))

Christina Smith was appointed principal flutist of the Atlanta Symphony in 1991, becoming at age 20 the youngest principal flutist of a major U.S. orchestra. She has appeared often as soloist with Atlanta and other orchestras, including the San Francisco Symphony. Smith regularly appears in recitals, chamber music performances, and masterclasses throughout the country. She serves on the faculty at Emory University and Kennesaw State University, both in Georgia. For more information, visit www.atlantasymphony.org.

When I was in high school, all I wanted was to go to the Curtis Institute of Music. I was an overachiever and practiced for hours and hours every day, until I got a really bad case of tendonitis during my senior year. The doctor told me, "You shouldn't play for several months." This was right before my college auditions.

I was absolutely devastated. I went to an arts medicine clinic, and they said, "Oh, you shouldn't play for the next year." I began worrying that I wouldn't be able to be a flutist — that I wouldn't be able to play again.

Around that time I met Keith Underwood, and I feel like he saved my life. I would not have a job today if not for him. Keith is the kind of person who can watch you play and say, "You have too much tension in your right shoulder and it completely changes your sound." His philosophy of playing centers around relaxation. He helped me with breathing techniques and he completely changed the way I play.

I went through a lot of physical therapy, and after several months away from the flute I started practicing a little, taking things really slow at first. Being the "type A" person that I was at the time, it was hard for me to play just five minutes a day, but I did it. I ended up getting into Curtis, and I went there for two years before I came to Atlanta.

That whole experience was a wakeup call for me — there was no way I could continue playing the way I'd played before. I've become absolutely obsessed with relaxation in playing, and I practice yoga. I also feel like the luckiest person in the world for meeting Keith Underwood when I did. Nowadays, I play over 200 concerts a year with the orchestra. If I was an uptight player like I was in high school, there's no way I would survive.

Joshua Smith)))

Joshua Smith is principal flute with the Cleveland Orchestra. He is head of the flute department at The Cleveland Institute of Music and appears internationally as a chamber musician and recitalist. For more information, check out his Web site at www.soloflute.com.

Nerves are something that a lot of musicians struggle with during performances. One of the questions I'm most often asked is: "How can I deal with nervousness, and how can I make it go away?" I don't think it ever really does go away. I can't think of anyone I've played with who doesn't find performing in front of people somewhat daunting.

Before a performance, we tend to think: "How I play today is a summation of who I am as a person and as a musician." We end up being too careful, trying to be perfect, trying not to miss a note. The creativity and spontaneity are gone because we're worried about what other people think rather than what we're doing in the moment.

What has often worked for me is to tell myself my performance is not for anyone except for the composer. If I'm playing a Mozart concerto, then the performance is for Mozart. The whole point is to figure out what he was trying to say when he wrote it down on paper, channel it, and communicate it to an audience, and that's hard enough. If I concentrate on how to do that well, then I'm not worried about anything else.

Jonathan Snowden)))

Jonathan Snowden has been principal flute of the Royal Philharmonic, London Philharmonic, and Philharmonia orchestras. He performs as soloist with orchestras and ensembles worldwide and has made numerous television appearances. Snowden has recorded extensively, including solo and orchestral repertoire, and work on film scores. He has also broadcast regularly for BBC Radio 3. Students come from all over the world to study with him at his home near Bath. For more information, visit www.jonathansnowden.com.

I started playing the flute at the age of 11. I had been going to a primary school where I was very happy and secure, but when I was 9 we had to move, and I ended up at a school which was quite rough. My parents had bought me a new flute, a silver-plated Gemeinhardt, which was really exciting, but I had to hide it every day in a big bag. All the rough boys were in gangs, and if you walked into school carrying a flute case, they attacked you.

I hated going to that school. I was artistic, and that didn't go down too well, but I gained a lot of prestige by winning a place in the rugby team. I was playing with the 17-year-olds when I was 14, because I could run fast. Then I was lucky enough to get into my county youth orchestra, which also met on Saturday mornings. I faced a stark dilemma, as rugby earned me credibility in my hostile school environment. I took a chance and opted for the flute, which cause me much anguish every Saturday.

However, there wasn't any doubt in my mind what I wanted to be. I remember going for a career interview when I was about 15, and they said, "What do you want to do?" I said, "I'm going to be first flute in a London orchestra." They said, "Oh, come on. Go work in a bank." I said, "No thanks." I left school when I was 16 and I went to the Guildhall School of Music in London, where I was finally able to start doing what I really wanted to do.

The flute is a fantastic instrument, a brilliant instrument. Unfortunately, it is often viewed as a feminine instrument. I didn't feel that way growing up, and I still don't. I think the most powerful music is expressed by balancing facets of both the masculine and feminine, structure and spirit. Music mirrors life's experiences, plus something else — magic!

Clare Southworth)))

A highly successful international soloist, Clare Southworth is also recognized as one of the United Kingdom's leading flute teachers. She taught for 17 years at the Royal Northern College of Music and is now professor of flute at the Royal Academy of Music in London. She has recorded two acclaimed CDs, and her books "Flute Aerobics," "Light Aerobics," and "Sequentials" are best-sellers. For more information, visit www.miyazawa.com or www.fluteconnection.net/contfl/contfl.html.

When I won first prize in the 1983 National Flute Association Competition, I thought that would open lots of doors for me. I really thought that was the answer — if you won an international competition, that was the beginning of your career.

I came back to England and wrote something like 600 letters — handwritten, because I didn't have a computer — to introduce myself to music clubs and other organizations where a musician could get work. I got about 10 replies, and only four concerts out of it. That was a reality check for me. Just because you've been quite successful at something, it doesn't necessarily mean that a lot will happen for you. It was a real struggle, though in one sense it was a good learning experience, because now I teach lots of students who think, "If only I can win this, win that, that'll do it." And it doesn't.

What gets you a career is continuous hard work and keeping people aware that you're around. I didn't do anything for a few years apart from writing those letters. I remember being very disappointed, very let down at the time because nobody seemed to be interested. And it wasn't really that they weren't interested — there just weren't any opportunities among those particular groups.

I was young and very naïve about the way things worked. After having won the competition, I didn't get back in touch with anyone from America because I didn't have any contacts — I didn't know who to write to. That was an opportunity lost. These days, because of the Internet, it's much easier to get in touch with people and make contacts, but in those days it was very hard.

I kept plugging away, auditioning, and writing letters, and eventually things got moving. I also set up a three-pronged attack to my career. At the time of the competition, I just had my playing, but since then I've really developed my teaching and my writing, which makes it easier to get work that involves all three. It all really came about through not giving up, and it's only been in the last 10 years or so that I've been going back to America, finally reaping the rewards from that competition 20 years ago.

Stuart Zolotorow

Mark Sparks)))

Acclaimed soloist, orchestral artist, chamber musician and teacher Mark Sparks was appointed principal flute of the St. Louis Symphony Orchestra in 2000. Sparks has performed with the New York Philharmonic, the Detroit and Baltimore symphonies, and held principal chairs in the San Antonio, Memphis, and Canton, Ohio symphony orchestras. He is on the faculty of the Aspen Music Festival, and has recorded a solo album for Summit Records. For more information, visit www.sparksflute.com.

My need communicate emotionally through music has kept me coming back to the practice room from the start. I've never thought of myself as super talented, but intuitive, determined, and completely committed to the music. I wanted to become principal flute of a major orchestra. Along the way I've had plenty of successes, but rejections, too.

I had great teachers. Robert Willoughby's musicianship and humanity, and Ransom Wilson's and Timothy Day's sounds in particular, were huge influences that I keep returning to. After conservatory I learned on my own. I tried to imitate Galway, Moyse, and many others through their recordings. Gradually, I discovered my own style.

The audition process was also a valuable self-teaching tool, and I loved the competition. I played principal in various orchestras, and kept learning through colleagues and experiences. Many days I played from the moment I woke until I turned out the light. Teaching others helped me learn and deepened my appreciation of life and flute playing.

However, my determination to become a principal in a major symphony was still to be tested. As associate principal in Baltimore, I realized I still had a lot to learn, but I became frustrated with the job. I felt estranged from the repertoire and marginalized from the orchestra. I tried to stay motivated through recording and other professional activities, but often I had to remind myself why I started playing in the first place. Sometimes I felt like a failure and seriously considered quitting. My family, especially my wife, was very helpful during this rather long period. Many colleagues were supportive. Luckily, I was teaching a lot. Through my students, I reinforced the motivational messages I was using myself:

- Work like a dog.

- Acknowledge the good things in your playing before dealing with the bad.

- Celebrate small successes.

- Have reasonable expectations of yourself and set short-term goals.

- Be a beginner every day so you remember the fundamentals.

- Keep it fun.

- Develop a hobby.

- Talk about your problems.

- Keep it in perspective; your problems are small, compared to those of many others.

Eventually, things went my way. Now, as principal flute of the St. Louis Symphony, I still find these are words to live by. And while I have found artistic fulfillment in my role at the heart of a great orchestra, I have found the desire to be excellent has only gotten stronger. Every day I am thankful for the opportunity to play, and to communicate through the flute.

Flute Stories

Alexa Still)))

Alexa Still is known internationally for her recordings on the Koch International Classics label, specializing in early twentieth-century repertoire. Her 10th solo CD, "Music of Sir Richard Rodney Bennett," was recently released. She is associate professor of flute at the University of Colorado at Boulder. Prior to this appointment she was principal flute of the New Zealand Symphony Orchestra. For more information, visit www.alexastill.com

I came from New Zealand to study in the States, and getting here was very hard financially. At one point I thought I wouldn't be able to do it. The exchange rate was something terrible, and New Zealand is not a wealthy country. Materially, people don't have as much as they do in the States.

I'd been teaching for years and doing things like picking strawberries to make money. I'd missed out on an Arts Council grant, which is the only way of getting a decent amount of money out of the New Zealand government, so I was feeling pretty depressed and sorry for myself.

Then, I got this check in the mail for a hundred dollars. It came with an anonymous note saying the person really loved hearing me play, wished me the best, and knew I would make it. Along with the note was this fantastic quote from Thoreau:

"I learned this, at least, by my experiment: that if one advances confidently in the direction of his dreams, and endeavors to live the life which he has imagined, he will meet with a success unexpected in common hours."

I still have that piece of paper framed on my desk. That vote of confidence from someone I didn't even know gave me the courage to keep working, playing concerts and recitals, and asking people for money, and in the end I managed to piece together enough to study in the States. If I hadn't made that trip, I sure as heck wouldn't play flute like I do now.

Flute Stories

Sheridon Stokes)))

Sheridon Stokes has taught flute at UCLA since 1972 and has recorded thousands of TV and movie soundtracks, including "Mission Impossible," "Jaws," and "Apollo 13." A three-time winner of the MVP award for flute from the National Academy of Arts & Sciences, he also received their Emeritus award in 1984. He has written numerous pieces for flute and is the author of "The Illustrated Method For Flute" and "Special Effects For Flute." For more information visit www.flute-music.com.

Having a career as a musician is not exactly cut and dry. You don't go through the usual process of getting a job, and it can get fairly discouraging at times. I had to deal with some difficult choices in my life when I was 25 and returning home from the Army.

When you get out of the Army, you're sort of lost — you just don't know who you are for awhile. I'd worked hard all my life — I'd been playing the flute since the age of 8, and I was hired as piccolo player for the Denver Symphony when I was 16 and still in high school. I'd been on the road, worked in Vegas, and at 20 was under contract for Alfred Newman in the 20th Century Fox Orchestra. When I was drafted, I played in the 7th Army Symphony in Germany, but after getting out I picked up my passport and kicked around Europe for awhile, just taking a vacation.

When I came back to L.A., I hadn't touched the flute in about six months. I didn't have any money, I was broke, and I had to figure out a way to support myself. I had to make decisions: Where am I going to go? What direction?

What I eventually discovered was that music was the most stable part of my life — it was actually a part of me, something I could turn to when things got tough. That realization was a turning point for me, and new things began to evolve. Until then I'd generally played along the lines of jazz and classical, but I started playing contemporary pieces and quickly found myself getting into modern music. I started composing, worked my way back into the studios, and began writing my flute method, which became popular over the years.

Music is a challenge, and to this day I'm always coming up with something new. I've taught at UCLA for 30 years, and the students really keep my mind going. I have no plans of retiring — it's just what I do. Over the years, dealing with marriages, mortgage payments, problems with kids, or anything, the music has always been there for me.

It's like a religion — it makes me feel good, and it's still the most stabilizing force in my life.

Flute Stories

Mary Stolper)))

Mary Stolper is principle flute of the Grand Park Symphony in Chicago and the Concertanti di Chicago Chamber Orchestra. She is the solo flutist for Chicago Opera Theater and the music ensemble Fulcrum Point, and chair of the flute faculty at DePaul University in Chicago. In addition to CD recordings, she has played for hundreds of TV and radio commercials. She may be contacted at mts310@aol.com.

As a student I never had specific goals to become an orchestral player or soloist. I never pigeonholed myself in any one direction. I just wanted to be the best I could be, and I thought the rest would take care of itself.

When I finished my masters degree, I experienced that horrible moment when you get out of school and say, "Now what do I do?" I'd been married since I was 19, and I had determined that I was going to make a career for myself in Chicago. I tried a couple of out-of-state auditions, but I don't think I fared very well at them because it was always in the back of my mind that I didn't want to leave the city or leave my husband.

No one at school prepares you for how hard it is to create work for yourself, and it's very difficult for college students to fathom what that's going to feel like. You also run up against the mentality that if you're not in a big orchestra, or someplace that gives you a credential, you must not be very good. Most students are never going to get an orchestral job, and they aren't adequately prepared for all the other opportunities out there in the musical field.

I taught a little and played some concerts, but I got overwhelmed by how difficult a career in music can be. Even worse, I found that certain doors were closed to me for reasons that had nothing to do with my flute playing. In the '70s, many people in the music world still did not take seriously a young, married women pursuing a career. This was despite the fact that I had just worked my way through grad school and killed myself getting straight-A's.

So for several years things looked bleak, and I felt like I was going to fade into the woodwork. I began to think, "Good flutists are a dime a dozen, and the world doesn't need another flute player. So why bother?" I packed up my flute and put it away.

I didn't play for about seven months, and then I got a call from my accompanist, who said, "This is really stupid. Get off your rear end and get back to work." So I did — I started plugging away again. And I decided to go to a masterclass taught by William Bennett.

I had always had to work during college, so I never went to festivals or masterclasses. No one ever encouraged me to apply to anything, and I lived in this little cocoon. So I went down to meet William Bennett and I was totally blown away. I found other people at his masterclass just like me, who hadn't won that great job in the sky by the time they were 23. Many of them were great players.

Bennett's masterclass put me around people who were creative, people who were working hard. It showed me that you can be extremely happy with your life, and with your flute playing, without the expectations of having to be one thing or another. I was interested again, and I started practicing heavily.

Then I got called to sub in Chicago's Grant Park Symphony. Also, right around that time, a flutist who played a lot of jobs around town got sick, and I got the call to play in her place. She never did come back to work, and that tragic event in her life became a door for me. From that one job I went to several others, and my career really began.

But if I'd gotten that call during the time in which I had quit, I wouldn't have prepared to meet the opportunity. It was William Bennett's masterclass that re-ignited my desire to get back into shape.

Jin Ta)))

Jin Ta joined the Singapore Symphony Orchestra as principal flutist in 1998. As a soloist, he has toured throughout the United States and Southeast Asia and has performed with numerous ensembles, including Israel's Haifa Chamber Orchestra, China's Shenzhen and Xiamen symphonies, and the U.S. Capital Wind Orchestra. He won first prize in the 2000 Haifa International Flute Competition in Israel. For more information, visit www.flutista.com.

When I was a student at the University of Michigan, the most difficult issue for me was my financial life — I was really poor. My years of studying in the States depended on scholarships, but for my living expenses I had to do all kinds of jobs. I worked at Pizza Hut and in a Japanese restaurant, served Chinese food, and flipped hamburgers. I've worked all positions in the food service industry, except manager.

One year I decided to enter the National Flute Association's Young Artist Competition. It was in Kansas that year, but I spent three months preparing for it at the Summer Festival in Breckenridge, Colorado. Then I took a bus to Kansas City.

The NFA competition ran for five days, and I had to share a two-bed hotel room with three other students. By the end, I didn't have much money left, and I put all my hopes on the idea that I'd win something and come home with some prize money. I advanced through all three rounds, and in the end I got a surprise — they issued me a check! My plan was to cash it right after the competition so I could buy myself a bus ticket back to Michigan, but that day was Saturday, and I discovered that all the downtown banks were closed.

So I sat in front of the hotel, watching all these flute players check out, and feeling really nervous. My friends had already gone. I didn't know anybody there. I had this check for $1,000 in my hands, but no place to cash it. And I had to get back to Michigan.

I found this guy I had met during the competition and made a deal with him, to trade my camera for $80 so I could buy a Greyhound ticket. I told him that as soon as I got back to Michigan I'd send him his money, so he could return my camera. Then I went to the Greyhound station.

To my surprise, a bus ticket from Kansas City to Michigan was over $80 — it was more like $120. I only had $88 in my pocket. This was really dangerous, because I was a foreign student and knew nobody in the States. I didn't know my way around Kansas City — I was in the middle of nowhere. I stood there staring at the ticket prices and thinking, "If I can't make it back to Michigan, God knows what will happen to me."

I'm not a very sociable guy, but I was really in a corner, so that pushed me to do whatever I had to do. I started talking to this guy who was some kind of station manager. We talked for two hours, and I found out his son was a University of Michigan grad and very involved in the football program. So I spent another hour talking to him about all the football games that had happened that year. By the end of our conversation, he gave me a special discount ticket for around $70.

The bus ride lasted about a day and a half. I was very hungry and thirsty, but I had a little money in my pocket for food, and above all I felt very happy that I could finally get myself back to Michigan.

It's very difficult to finish your studies as a music major in the States. Financial difficulty is like a shadow, always following you. Many times I thought about quitting and switching my major to computer science, because it would be easier to get a job. Many of my friends, also flutists, did change their majors. But I believed in myself — I trusted my ability as a flute player to help me reach my goal, and that's what kept me going all those years.

Flute Stories

Dave Valentin)))

Dave Valentin was awarded a Grammy in 2003 for best Latin jazz album with collaborator Dave Samuels, for their Caribbean Jazz Project album "The Gathering." Valentin was nominated for best R&B instrumentalist in 1985. He has made nearly two dozen of his own albums and appeared on many more, performing with musicians like percussionist Tito Puente, pianist McCoy Tyner, and jazz flutist Herbie Mann. For more information on Valentin and his recordings, check out www.concordrecords.com/bios/valentin.html.

Being accepted into the jazz community as a Puerto Rican wasn't easy at first. I grew up in the South Bronx at a time when we Puerto Rican musicians were just coming onto the scene. We were street people, with a warrior's attitude toward our music: "Yo, we're not going away." But to get into the jazz circle, we really had to prove to the old-timers that we could play.

We also had to convince the Puerto Rican and Hispanic community. They always said, "Why don't you play salsa?" I kept telling them, "I already did that." Eventually, little by little, they understood.

In those days, the only way you could learn — not only in jazz but in

Latin music as well — was by sitting in with the old-timers. I remember going to a jazz club in the Bronx at 1 in the morning with trumpet and conga player Jerry Gonzales. I sat in onstage, and after the set this old-timer asked me, "What's your name?" I said, "David Valentin." He said, "Do me a favor. Go home and learn the changes."

So I came back six months later to the same club and sat in again. And the same man asked me, "What's your name?" I said, "David Valentin." He said, "Why don't you go home and learn the melody?"

So I did. And a while later, I had the courage to go back again. After the set, the very same old-timer turned to me and said, "Dave, you sounded good."

Guys like him weren't trying to discourage me, they just told me the truth. If you're going to play "I Love You Porgy," you have to learn the parts. And as an instrumentalist, you have to listen to vocalists — everyone who ever sang it, whether it's Billie Holiday or Tony Bennett or whoever — just to learn the phrasing.

Most of all, you have to have the passion. In those days, my apartment consisted of a sofa bed and a fish tank with no fish. I ate pizza for two years. Without the passion, you're going to be in a lot of trouble, because in music you have to sacrifice almost everything to get to where you want to be — and you don't even know whether you're going to get there.

Tito Puente once told us, "If you're tired, stay home. If you can't walk, sit down. If you can't drive, don't. But if you play with me, you got to play." That goes for everything in life — if you're going to sit home and complain about the situation, you're wasting your time. If you're going to be a father, play. If you're going to be a friend, play. If you're going to be a teacher, play. And if you're going to be a musician, play. It's not just a job — you have to get out there and get involved.

Jim Walker)))

Jim Walker's artistry reaches extensively into the worlds of orchestral and chamber music, improvisational jazz, motion picture soundtracks, and numerous recordings both as a solo artist and with his jazz-classical group Free Flight. He lectures full-time at the University of Southern California Thornton School of Music. For more information, visit www.jimwalkerflute.com.

As a high school student I was very interested in jazz, but I came to understand that I didn't have what it took to become great at improvising. My father was a musician who had the magic touch as an improviser, but I had to come to grips with the fact that I did not, and I suffered a lot of discouragement from that. In fact, when I got to college I decided to put away my jazz ambitions and focus on other things.

I suffered another musical setback during my senior year in college. I took some lessons with a teacher who, to put it mildly, was not encouraging — to the point that he squelched any ambition I had at all for becoming a professional player. I know it was not his intention to do that, but by the end of my senior year I had no thoughts of becoming an orchestral player or a recording artist. And certainly not a jazz player. I got into the West Point band the following year, but I still suffered from a sort of lethargy.

I was a year into my Army tenure when a moment of truth finally hit me. I just realized I had to make a decision — was I going to become a flute player or stay in the Army the rest of my life? So I decided to start practicing.

At that time, the Army made funds available for private lessons, and I was lucky enough to take lessons with Harold Bennett, who was principal flutist of the Metropolitan Opera Orchestra. He was the right medicine at the right time for me. With Bennett's help, I started feeling like I could really play the flute. I began to believe I might actually be competitive in the auditions circuit. And in fact, at the end of that year I took an audition at the Pittsburgh Symphony and got the job as associate principal flutist.

So I became a symphonic player. But it wasn't until eight years later that I finally began to confront that improvisation demon. I became aware of the Jamey Aebersold improvisation book/play-along record series, which takes you through the learning process step by step, and after several years of practice I actually did become an improviser.

There are times when you question your ability, and you wonder whether your dreams will ever be fulfilled, but ultimately your level of achievement, and your level of discouragement, is up to you. Don't ever let anyone talk you out of becoming something you want to be. And don't wait for someone to talk you into following your dreams.

Flute Stories

Brooks de Wetter-Smith)))

Brooks de Wetter-Smith has appeared as a soloist and has presented masterclasses throughout the United States, Europe, the Middle East, South America, and Asia. He teaches at the University of North Carolina at Chapel Hill and is past president of the National Flute Association. He has released recordings on a number of labels, as well as recording for PBS, Radio Bremen, Bavarian Radio, Salzburg Radio, and Radio/Television Hong Kong. For more information, visit www.unc.edu/~brooks.

One of my most unusual experiences was performing in the Occupied Territories in the West Bank (Palestine). I was asked by the U.S. State Department, which supports cultural exchanges around the world, to go up to An-Najah University in Nablus and do a program on improvisation.

Because I was living in the West Bank and in Israel proper, I spent a lot of time with Palestinians, and I felt very safe and comfortable with them. I've traveled the region, been in Arab buses, met with families, and always felt welcomed. But when I went to Nablus, the State Department insisted on taking me up there in an armored car, with bullet-proof glass and sides. It was amazing to have to travel like that to a place I was generally familiar with.

When we got to the university, I realized not long into my presentation that the students were watching my instrument very intently. Someone finally mentioned to me that no one there had ever seen a modern flute up close. They'd seen flutes on television and in films, but here it was 1997, and these Palestinians had never actually seen a modern flute. To me, it seemed unbelievable.

After the program, several musicians in the audience wanted to share their music with me. One started playing an oud, a traditional Arab lute. It was captivating. Here I was, suddenly in the same shoes they'd been in an hour earlier — being introduced to an instrument that I had heard of, but had never actually listened to, nor seen.

We discussed the elements of improvisation in Arabic and Western music, and I became really intrigued by those differences, so I went back to the Middle East in '99. I spent half a year there and worked with an Arabic improvisation group called Sabreen, and over that time I began to sense, in a strong way, a kind of unity we shared through the music.

Flute music is nonverbal, but it communicates a sense of humanity that crosses cultural borders. With all this warmongering going on — and with all the difficulties that the Western world seems to perceive with the Arab world, and vice versa — it's important to step back and realize we feel the same feelings, breathe the same air, bleed the same blood. Music is a means for recognizing these common experiences.

There's something much larger to the purpose of music and flute playing than just getting the right notes and playing nice music. I've been in Lebanon, Syria, Jordan. I've played for the Chinese, Japanese, Russians, Czechs, Brazilians. Swedes, and many others as well. While the world is so focused on what divides us, music is a great symbol of what can unite us. It's a way of affirming our mutual humanity — the dignity that all mankind shares.

I don't know of a better way that I could be active in communicating this humanity across cultural borders. For me, music carries a sense of humanitarian commitment, and when you really feel in sync with something that you're doing, it's no longer work. It's personal fulfillment. It's an extension of who you are.

Robert Willoughby)))

Robert Willoughby has received the National Flute Association Lifetime Achievement Award. He serves on the faculty at the Longy School of Music in Boston and taught previously at Oberlin Conservatory and the Peabody Conservatory of Music. He has served as principal flutist of the Cincinnati Symphony and played with the Cleveland Orchestra. He has toured internationally, made numerous recordings, and teaches modern and baroque flute. He may be contacted at macandbob@compuserve.com.

At the end of my senior year in high school, I was at Interlochen Music Camp. My teacher, Larry Torno, who was first flutist of the St. Louis Symphony, suggested that I play for the director of the Eastman School of Music, Dr. Howard Hanson. At a meeting of the entire camp that evening it was announced that I had won a full scholarship to Eastman.

The next morning I played first flute in the orchestra — we were playing the Polovtsian Dances by Borodin, which I wasn't too familiar with. There's a lovely flute solo in one spot, but unbeknownst to me, the second flute enters two beats before the first flute. I heard the second flute begin, and figuring I must have miscounted, I skipped two beats and began to play.

The conductor, who was a big burly Russian from the Pittsburgh Symphony, stopped the orchestra, looked over his glasses, and shouted two words: "Scholarship, bah!"

Needless to say, I wasn't exactly thrilled. But I was one of two flutists who chaired the first spot in the orchestra that summer, so I knew I wasn't a bad player. I determined I wasn't going to let one small bump in the road keep me from doing my best. There would be other bumps.

Later on, while studying for my master's degree at the New England Conservatory of Music, I practiced particularly hard one week for my lesson with Georges Laurent, who was then first flutist of the Boston Symphony, as well as my idol. Arriving for my lesson, I was asked to play the one thing I hadn't spent much time on. After I played, Mr. Laurent turned to me, and in a stern voice said, "What's the matter, haven't you been practicing?"

The rest of the lesson went well, but after that I was so depressed. I walked around a pond near his home for about half an hour to regain my composure. And I determined that never again would he find it necessary to ask such a question. Whether it's for a lesson or an audition, you just can't afford to leave anything out, because you never know what will be asked of you.

I've been in the music business now for about 60 years. I still love playing and teaching, and despite the occasional bump in the road, I can't imagine a more satisfying profession.

Ransom Wilson)))

In addition to performing as solo flutist with major orchestras around the world, Ransom Wilson is also an orchestral conductor of growing reputation. He is founder and conductor of the Solisti New York Orchestra and has been guest conductor for many prestigious ensembles. Wilson has recorded 30 albums as both flutist and conductor and has been nominated for three Grammy awards. He recently formed a new CD label, Image Recordings. For more information visit www.ransomwilson.com.

I'm from Tuscaloosa, Alabama, a small town in the South. When I was starting high school there, it was in general a very racist and conformist place. My family were Unitarians and integrationists — two things which were anathema to many people in that town. Going to class we were called names, and rocks were thrown at us. When it became obvious that I was good at playing flute, I quickly realized it was my ticket out of town.

My mother saw a small article in the newspaper — the North Carolina School of the Arts was looking for talented students throughout the country. I jumped at it, and within a few months I was gone. I've never really been back for any length of time.

My flute teacher in North Carolina was Philip Dunigan. He was a student of both William Kincaid and Julius Baker, so he had some really interesting things to say about the flute. He instilled in the entire class a sense that music was vital to a life with meaning, and he said something that I felt was profound — he never wanted any of his students to sound like him, and he never wanted us to sound like each other. He encouraged us to find our individual voices, instead of being part of a sausage-making machine, and I'm very grateful for that. He was also the first person to introduce me to Jean-Pierre Rampal, though Dunigan didn't know him personally.

Our class went to two Rampal concerts in New York. I'd never even heard of the guy, since I was from Alabama, so I bought an LP of him playing the Quantz concertos. It was the most astonishing thing I'd ever heard. We went to the concerts, and I remember my mouth dropping open when I heard the first note. It was so alive — I'd never heard anyone play that way before.

The next year, Rampal actually came to play in North Carolina, and we had an opportunity to go backstage and meet him. I told him I wanted to study with him in Nice, because I knew he taught a class there. Rampal looked at me and said, "How long have you been playing?" I said very proudly, "For four years." And he said, "Oh, well, I have an assistant." It really upset me. I punished him by not playing his albums for a month.

But later in New York I got to meet him again, and after I played for him, he said, "You must come to Nice." So I went to Nice and it changed my life. (Nowadays, I myself teach every summer in Nice.)

When I got there, I played the F-minor Telemann sonata for him. I had heard him play it in concerts and knew it was one of his favorite pieces.

He corrected me immediately on the Americanism which he called "dah DAH." It's an unnatural elongation and emphasis on the pickup to the bar, and I suspect that it comes from jazz or some kind of pop music.

The second thing he told me was that I kept cracking middle register E. It was to become my greatest nemesis in my playing — even today, if I'm not careful, I'll just crack E. But he asked me why I was doing it, and in an uncharacteristic moment of clarity, I said my first words in French to him, which translated as "I'm afraid." I don't know what made me say that. He affected me so deeply that I actually admitted the truth — and just admitting that in front of the great master helped me changed my relationship to the instrument.

Years later, Rampal and I played a number of concerts together. It's hard to convey what magic was in his playing — it was the reason audiences from any culture flocked to him. On our very last tour together, I purposefully put the F-minor sonata by Telemann on the program. During the performances, I would always do the "dah DAH" — just the way I had done it when I first got to Nice and played it for him. Then I'd look over to Rampal, and he would laugh.

Cori Wells Braun

Carol Wincenc)))

Carol Wincenc teaches flute at The Juilliard School and at the State University of New York in Stony Brook. She has appeared as soloist with major orchestras worldwide and premiered works written for her by many prominent composers. She is a prolific recording artist, and music publisher Carl Fischer has created a series of Carol Wincenc Signature Editions, featuring her favorite flute repertoire. For more information, visit www.trawickartists.net/acts/carol_wincenc.html.

My father was a symphony conductor, and he was actually my first music teacher — on the violin. From the time I was 4, the sound of the violin was planted in my brain. The friction, resonance, and physicality of the bow all made a lasting impression on me.

When I was 9, the people running the music program at my school asked, "What instrument do you want to play?" I chose the flute because it meant I could play in the band, which was very important to me. Also, I thought the flute seemed feminine and very pretty. I demonstrated a gift for it right away, and I had a pretty good, rich sound because I modeled it after the violin. By the time I was 15, I knew I was heading for a professional career.

There are things I don't like about the flute. I feel a limitation with it, in that I can't get the power that I could from the bow, the voice, or the piano. Those are strong instruments in the orchestra. You can play the flute with power but it takes a lot of development, and as an instrument it's just "lighter" by nature.

But in retrospect, I'm glad I picked the flute. I love the agility and the physicality of it. The act of breathing into an instrument is both healing and gratifying. Most of all, I love its vocal qualities — the flute is very close to the human voice.

It's fulfilling for me. But it's not just the flute, it's everything that comes with it: Having an active performing career. Being a teacher. Being a mom. I'm very grateful to work in my field because I'm always surrounded by people striving for excellence and involved in the creation of high art. That's important during a time when our culture is struggling to hang on to something of enduring value. Governments crumble, the world changes; art alone endures. Playing music and playing the flute are important parts of a fulfilling life.

John Wion)))

John Wion served as principal flutist of the New York City Opera from 1965 to 2002. He is professor of flute and chamber music at The Hartt School, University of Hartford, in Connecticut. In addition to his international career as a soloist, he has recorded extensively and published a nine-volume series of opera excerpt books for flutists. For more information, visit http://johnwion.com.

I began playing the fife in a school band in Melbourne, Australia, because my older brothers had done so, and I started studying the flute when I was ten. In 1958, when I was twenty one, I came to New York to study with Julius Baker and later with Claude Monteux. I also began working at The Waldorf Astoria, running elevators, and my boss, Mr. Thomas, was encouraging me to train as a hotel executive.

By 1960 I was studying with Monteux, and he started giving me some of the jobs and teaching that he couldn't cover. I played some school concerts with a soprano and harpist in Baltimore. No sooner back from that, I was taking my weekly lesson when the phone rang. It was Joe DeAngelis, personnel manager of the New York Philharmonic. The NYP was doing Mahler's Ninth and needed five flutes — was Claude available for the next week's concerts? No, he wasn't. He was playing the "Rite of Spring" with The Symphony of the Air, Toscanini's old NBC Orchestra. Did Claude know anyone at all who was free? Claude handed me the phone, and in a daze I wrote down the necessary information.

Mr. Thomas at The Waldorf was not about to give me a week off, particularly if he knew the reason for it. So I quit my job and went to hire a set of tails. I was a musician again.

Incredibly, here I was on the stage of Carnegie Hall in all its cream, gold, and red velvet glory — the legendary John Wummer offstage playing long tones into the wall, Music Director Leonard Bernstein backstage saying a friendly hello, the aging, bald-headed Dmitri Mitropoulis conducting my debut in Mahler's great Ninth Symphony. The second flute was Bob Morris, third was Paige Brook, and Frances Blaisdell was substituting for an ailing Fred Heim.

Thursday evening I got into my outfit — dress shirt, studs, wing collar, and bow tie. Upstairs in the orchestra's dressing room I walked around trying to look nonchalant. One of the members came up to me and said, "Who are you?" I told him, and he waved at my attire, saying, "I thought you must be out front." I looked more carefully at everyone and saw to my great embarrassment that they all just wore regular white shirts with clip-on bow ties.

Somehow I survived the evening, and for the following performances I came properly dressed. Much later I learned that this season's Mahler concerts constituted the revival which put him firmly in the Philharmonic's repertoire. As for myself, it was a remarkable week and an auspicious beginning.

Flute Stories

Trevor Wye)))

Trevor Wye teaches a residential course for post-graduate students and plays concerts throughout the world, including his unique recital "flutes fantastic!" in which he plays on more than 50 different flutes. He has made several solo recordings and is author of the world-famous "Practice Books" series for flute, among other publications. Wye has taught at the Guildhall School of Music, London, and the Royal Northern College of Music in Manchester. For more information, visit www.trevor-wye.com.

I was very interested in science at school, and whenever there wasn't a science subject, I usually took the day off — though my mother didn't know about this. On one of those days, as I was getting ready to go to a museum, I heard a flute player on the radio. It suddenly struck me: "I want to do that." But it wasn't the sound of the flute that interested me. It was the sound of the fingers stopping the holes.

A while later I heard a clarinet playing the variation in the "Young Person's Guide to the Orchestra" by Benjamin Britten — the bit that goes whizzing up and down in arpeggios. That attracted me for the same reason.

But when I heard a flutist playing the "Chinese Dance" from the Nutcracker suite, that clinched it. I decided, "I've got to play the flute."

It wasn't the sound of the fingers themselves, but the little "click" sounds of the notes changing. I was fascinated by sounds like that. I remember whistling down a vacuum cleaner tube to hear the notes changing very quickly, like a horn player running through the harmonic scale on one breath. My sister would say, "Are you having lessons on the vacuum cleaner yet?"

So it was the acoustics of it that got me started on flute, and I ended up taking private lessons, though I never attended a conservatory or music school. By the time I was 26 and already started on my career, I decided to take a class in Switzerland with Marcel Moyse. I went there thinking, "This will be fun, and I'll get a lot out of it." But when I played for him I found that some of the things he was teaching were completely new for me, and that I was obviously running up the wrong track.

It was quite a shock for me, and a turning point in my life. I remember leaving in the middle of the course and going down to Lucerne, where I went up a mountain and just sat there. When I came back the next day, Moyse said, "You were not here yesterday." I said, "No." He asked, "What were you doing?" "Thinking," I said. And he replied, "Oh, I understand."

After three or four days, I realized what his message was: Stop playing the flute and play the music. It turned everything I knew on its head. I had thought the way to play the flute was just to let everything go — to put everything you can into it. What I realized was, you have to be a little more intelligent than that. My realization didn't change my enjoyment of playing, but it changed my enjoyment of listening. Most of the players I'd been worshipping simply let everything go, and I no longer found that very interesting.

I love the flute and enjoy what I do very much. Since those lessons with Moyse, I'm just much more picky about what I like and don't like.

Anne Diener Zentner)))

Anne Diener Zentner is principle flute with the Los Angeles Philharmonic. She has served on the faculty at the University of Southern California and at Rice University in Houston, Texas. She may be contacted at adzentner@yahoo.com.

The summer I was 16, my teacher suggested that I audition for a well-known flute player on the East Coast. This was someone I looked up to at that time — a flutist who had gone through many difficulties in getting their position — and I wanted very much to meet this person and study with them.

My father wrote and asked if I could have an audition, and this flutist agreed. When we arrived after a long drive from Buffalo, New York, no one was there to meet us. My father was ill with pneumonia, and we waited two hours in the rain, but this flutist never showed up. We finally tracked them down at a concert that evening, and they agreed to hear me play. I was an unbelievably shy kid, so it was very hard for me to play in front of my idol, but I finally had my chance.

My audition took place in what was basically a restroom backstage. After half a page I was stopped and told that I really had no talent. This person told me there was no way I could ever make a living playing the flute. I should forget an orchestral career and focus on something outside of music.

I was absolutely devastated. I decided I would give up the flute, and I packed it away and didn't touch it for about six weeks that summer.

In the end, I picked up the flute again because I realized I had to. I couldn't imagine existing without playing. What pulled me through was very strong support from both my family and my teachers. But that terrible rejection always hurt, and it ultimately gave me a strong sense of obligation toward the students I would one day be teaching, because you never know how much weight your words are going to carry. The important thing is to give guidance and direction without squashing somebody.

When I met this flute player many years later, after I had been appointed principle flute at the Los Angeles Philharmonic, they claimed not to remember me at all. I found that strange.

As for myself, the people I'll always remember are the ones who encouraged me and told me not to give up.

Flute Stories

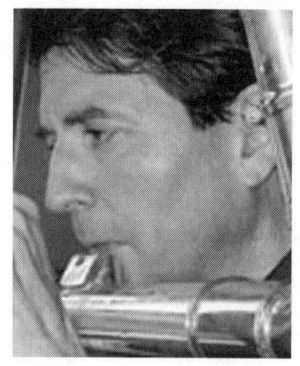

Matthias Ziegler)))

Matthias Ziegler is one of the world's most versatile and innovative flutists, committed to playing and composing contemporary music, and broadening the expressive potential of traditional flutes and the electroacoustically amplified contrabass flute. He is principal flutist with the Collegium Novum Zurich, professor at the Zurich Conservatory, and performs internationally with many great musicians and ensembles. For more information about Ziegler and his solo CD "Uakti," available on New Albion Records, visit http://newalbion.com/na104 or www.matthias-ziegler.ch.

I studied both architecture and music while attending university, but when I was 21 or 22 my feelings for the flute got so strong that I decided music was the direction I would go. For me, that was an important decision.

I had played flute since I very was young. I also began playing drums, guitar, and saxophone, and I developed a big interest in improvised music. While I was studying classical music, I was in the jazz clubs a lot playing standards. I played big band and even went on tour with a pop group. All these styles and elements would later influence my recordings, but at 22, I said, "Okay, I'm just going to focus on the flute."

I played for Conrad Klemm, a teacher at the Zurich Conservatory, and he said, "You can study with me, but I won't let you play like this. We have to step back and talk about the fundamentals of flute technique." That was very difficult for me, because in my head, my attitude, and my musical ideas, I was further advanced than that. I wanted to say, "Let me play, let me run." But Klemm told me, "Don't think in terms of years, think in terms of 10 years. And just imagine where you'll arrive if you follow these ideas for 10 years."

So for at least a year I did almost no performance. I just tried to build up a basic technique. It was hard work, but with Klemm's help I stopped being an "end-gainer" — looking for immediate results. I learned to take little steps.. After awhile, I could look back and see where those steps had led me in my musical development. When I thought about what he had said 10 years later, I was able to say, "That worked out perfectly."

While I was doing this technical work, I didn't want to stop my creative motor, so I continued to play improvised music on my own. That was my personal field — I was trying to find and develop my own language. It helped a lot that my musical background went beyond just flute scales and flute technique.

The whole attitude of not being an end-gainer can lead you to find your best qualities after awhile. You just follow your intuition, and the difficulties you go through often give you good tools to help you develop your own music, your own voice. Instead of thinking, "How many CDs will I sell?" or "How many people will listen to my concerts?" you follow your own way of playing the music, and find people who like it.

There is risk in taking such a noncommercial attitude, but trying to be commercial is just as much a risk, since a very small peak of artists make the big money in the commercial field. Following your own street is a very strong feeling, and for me there was never a choice. It's the only way I function.

Flute Stories

Laurel Zucker)))

Laurel Zucker is professor of flute at California State University, Sacramento, and a recording artist with 21 CDs on Cantilena Records, including her most recent release, "Telemann Fantasies." Zucker is a Miyazawa Artist, a past Artists International Competition winner, winner of the American Music Center's Aaron Copeland Award, and recipient of the President's Award for research and creativity at CSUS. For a full listing of her recordings, visit www.fluteworld.com

My first semester at the New England Conservatory, I slipped on a Boston street and broke my hand — a really bad break. I used to love running outside, and that day I didn't notice the black ice.

The first doctor I went to told me my hand would be paralyzed. I was horrified, so I called my father. He had gone to school at MIT, and I hoped he might have some friends who could refer me to someone else. And he did. The second doctor re-set my hand, and it eventually healed fine.

It put me out of commission my first semester at the conservatory. That was a drag, but I never felt like quitting. I spent a huge amount of time studying symphony scores, listening to a lot of music, and socializing, so the semester turned out to be very fruitful for me. The next semester I started playing again. It was hard because I hadn't practiced in awhile, and it was painful getting the use of my hand back. But I pulled it off and went on after that to study at Juilliard.

Much later, during my eighth year of teaching at Cal State Sacramento, that same hand started giving me terrible trouble again. It was my left index finger, at the joint — the same area where it had been broken. I didn't know what was going on, but it got so painful that I started thinking that maybe I should get another career.

I spent a year going to several specialists, including top surgeons in New York, and they all told me my problem was very serious and complex. Finally I found a hand surgeon who said, "You have bone spurs from when you broke your hand." This guy was cocky, but I trusted him because he was the only specialist who told me, "It's really a simple operation. It'll be fully cured in a week." So I had the surgery and my hand has been fantastic ever since.

But this time around, the experience forced me to think about what I would do if I couldn't play the flute. I considered trying administration or getting more into composition. I could become a band director at a public school or try conducting at a college. Rather than worry too much, I began to focus on the other possibilities.

I realized there are always choices. My first choice is to play the flute, but there are always ways to surround yourself with music and keep it in your life.

Flute Stories

Eugenia Zukerman)))

Eugenia Zukerman has performed as a soloist and with orchestras and ensembles throughout the world. She has made numerous recordings and is artistic director of the international Vail Valley Music Festival, Colorado. Zukerman has been the arts correspondent for "CBS News' Sunday Morning" since 1981 and is an author of both novels and nonfiction works, including "Coping With Prednisone" (St. Martin's Press), co-authored with her sister, Dr. Julie R. Ingelfinger. For more information, visit www.eugeniazukerman.com.

In 1994, I discovered I had a life-threatening lung disease. It was very frightening because I had been feeling like I couldn't breathe very well and that I had a slight cough, but at first no doctors could find anything wrong. When I finally went in for X rays, they found I had a rare disease which was not contagious, because it wasn't caused by a virus or bacteria. It was just my body acting upon itself.

I took heavy doses of a drug called Prednisone for more than a year. It saved my life, but the medication has enormous side effects. The effects can be physical, but they're also psychological. I was very paranoid at the time and subject to panic attacks. My sister, Julie Ingelfinger — a doctor at Harvard — helped me strategize ways of avoiding the side effects whenever possible. I didn't want people to know what I was going through, because who's going to hire a flutist with a lung disease?

It was ultimately the flute that got me through. They say music is a path between ourselves and the infinite, and in a way I really felt that. It was my lifeline, connecting me to a healing process — particularly when I played Bach or Mozart, just for myself. Listening to the CDs and concerts of other people helped me as well.

As soon as I started taking the medication I could breathe better, and I was able to keep playing. I had a very heavy schedule, and it was all very difficult because of the high doses. I did have some setbacks. What really inspired me to stay on the regime was the idea that if I took the medication, I would be able to go on playing the flute.

My father had died just the year before, and I was extremely close to him. I had a dream that he came to me, and I was depressed in the dream — I told him I was tired and that I didn't think I could do this. And he gave me his beautiful smile and said, "Your work is not done."

I think as flutists we take it for granted that we'll be able to go on playing as long as we like. I've been fine now for years, and I think I will continue to be fine, but realizing that you might have to stop doing something you love makes that thing all the more precious to you. I know now how important the flute is to me.

index)))

A)

Abeshouse, Adam, 190
Abrahams, Mick, 2
Academia Wind Ensemble, 48
A.D.D. Trio, 72
Aeolian Chamber Players, 102
American Composers Orchestra, 159
Andersen, Joachim, 144
Anderson, Ian, 1, 127-28
An-Najah University, Nablus, 218
Arcata String Quartet, 8
Arnheim, Yossi, 4
Asbjørnsen, Lars, 6
Aspen Music Festival Orchestra, 8, 37, 183, 201
Atlanta Symphony Orchestra, 171, 193
Atlantic Sinfonietta, 93
Atlantic Symphony, 124
Aureole, 95

B)

Bach, Carl Philipp Emanuel, 89
Bach, Johann Sebastian, 45, 48, 54, 96, 104, 160, 239
Bach Aria Group, 95
Bach Chamber Soloists, 159
Bach Orchestra, 8
Bailey, Don, 8
Baker, Julius, 10, 16, 36, 53, 94, 97-98, 101, 134, 136, 185, 224, 228
Baltimore Symphony Orchestra, 65, 142, 179, 190, 201-2
Barge Chamber Series, 188
Baron, Samuel, 96
Barone, Clement, 12, 122, 136
Barrere, Georges, 30-31
Barry, John, 73
Bartók, Béla, 74
Bartoli, Cecilia, 94

Basel Radio Symphony Orchestra, 156
Baxtresser, Jeanne, 14, 188
Beach Boys, the, 184
Beatles, the, 80, 127
Beethoven, Ludwig van, 100, 124-25, 140, 190
Belgian National Opera Orchestra, 111
Belgian Radio and Television Symphony Orchestra, 111
Belolavec, Jiri, 89
Bengtson, Janne, 17
Bennett, Harold, 191-92, 217
Bennett, Sir Richard Rodney, 204
Bennett, Tony, 215
Bennett, William, 20, 60, 140-41, 144, 209-10
Benny Andersson's (ABBA) Band, 19
Berg, Alban, 140
Berg, Jacob, 23
Berkenstock, Jean, 25
Berlin Philharmonic Orchestra, 156, 162-63
Berlin Symphony, 81
Bernstein, Leonard, 179, 189, 229
Beynon, Emily, 27
Birmingham Conservatoire, 78
Birmingham Symphony Orchestra, City of, 39
Bishop, Henry, 82
Blaisdell, Frances, 29, 229
Bolshoi Ballet, 149, 151
Borodin, Alexander, 221
Boston Symphony Orchestra, 34-35, 65, 120, 140, 222
Bothy Band, The, 147-48
Boukobza, Laurent, 46
Boulez, Pierre, 118, 189
Bournemouth Symphony Orchestra, 60

Boustany, Wissam, 32
Bowman, Randolph, 34
Boyd, Bonita, 37, 192
Boyd-Goluses Duo, 37
Brahms, Johannes, 77, 125, 165, 188
Breckenridge Summer Festival, 211
Breidenthal, Dave, 74
Brentano Quartet, 95
Bright Sheng, 75
Britten, Benjamin, 230
Brook, Paige, 229
Brooklyn College, 99
Buffalo Philharmonic, 23
Bychkov, Semyon, 43

C)

Campbell, Margaret, 39
Cantin, Catherine, 42
Canton Symphony Orchestra, Ohio, 201
Carnegie-Mellon University, 58
Carpathian Basin Street Band, 137
Carribbean Jazz Project, 214
Casals Festival, 113
Casals, Pablo, 99-100, 103
CBS Orchestra, 10
Central City Colorado Opera Festival, 58
Chamber Music Society of Lincoln Center, 188
Chambers, Celia, 44
Chastain, Kathleen, 46
Chautauqua Symphony Orchestra, 50, 166
Cherry, Ann, 48
Chicago College of Performing Arts, Roosevelt University, 25
Chicago Opera Theater, 208
Chicago Symphony Orchestra, 10, 129, 140, 164-65, 183

index

Chicago Youth Orchestra, 25-26
Chieftains, the, 146, 148
China National Symphony, 4
Chopin, Frédéric, 76
Church, Sandra, 50
Cincinnati College-Conservatory of Music, University of, 93
Cincinnati Symphony Orchestra, 23, 34-35, 221
Clark, Kenny, 137
Clapton, Eric, 1, 3
Cleveland Institute of Music, 48, 195
Cleveland Symphony Orchestra, 10, 48, 58, 124-25, 195, 221
Coelho, Tadeu, 52
Cole, Robert, 55
College-Conservatory of Music, University of Cincinnati, 34
Collegium Novum Zurich, 234
Collegium Vocale of St. Louis, 23
Colorado at Boulder, University of, 204
Colvig, David, 136
Columbus Symphony, 152
Composers Quartet, Maine, 152
Concertanti di Chicago Chamber Orchestra, 208
Copland, Aaron, 175
Cramer, David, 58
Curtis Institute of Music, The, 10-11, 56, 58-59, 124, 136, 193

D)

Dallas Chamber Orchestra, 8
Dallas Symphony, 181
Danish Ballet, 151
Darden, George, 118
Davies, Gareth, 60
Davies, Philippa, 63
Davis, Miles, 135

Day, Timothy, 65, 201
DeAngelis, Joe, 229
Debost, Michel, 47, 68, 144
Debussy, Claude, 20, 95, 100, 165
Denver Symphony Orchestra, 186, 206
DePaul University, Chicago, 164, 208
DeRosa, Vincent, 73
Detroit Symphony Orchestra, 12, 122-23, 149, 166, 186, 201
Dick, Robert, 70
Di Tullio, Joseph, 73
Di Tullio, Louise, 73
Doppler, Albert Franz, 145
Dorough, Aralee, 75
Drexler, George, 114, 184
Dufrene, Fernand, 21
Dunigan, Philip, 224
Durán, Elena, 78

E)

Eastman School of Music, The, 10, 37, 120, 130, 191-92, 221
East Wind, flute and harp duo, 4
Eisen, Steve, 127-28
Emory University, 193
Ephross, Arthur, 53
Epstein, Moshe Aron, 81
Eschenbach, Christoph, 75-77
Estrin, Harvey, 119
Evanston Symphony, 26

F)

Fauré, Gabriel, 61, 118
Filharmonica della Scala, 86
Findon, Andy, 84
Finnish Radio Symphony Orchestra, 139
Fischer, Edwin, 104
Fischer-Dieskau, Dietrich, 37

Fisher, John, 57
Florio, Ermanno, 172
Folkwanghochschule, 7
FOReM, 106
Formisano, Davide, 86
Fort Wayne Philharmonic, 179
Foster, Lawrence, 114
France, Orchestre National de, 89
Francis, John, 143-44
Franck, César, 14
Frank, Evelyn, 61
Free Flight, 216
Frisland Symphony Orchestra, 89
Fulcrum Point, 208
Fullerton, California State University, 73
Furtwangler, Wilhelm, 104

G)

Gallois, Patrick, 88
Galway, James, 91, 94, 134, 144, 201
Garner, Bradley, 93
Garner, Gary, 93
Gazzelloni, Severino, 49
Geneve, Conservatoire de, 156
Giger, Paul, 72
Gilbert, Geoffrey, 20-21, 144-45
Gilbert, Laura, 95
Godard, Benjamin, 145
Goff, Scott, 97
Goldberg, Bernard, 99
Goldsmith, Jerry, 73
Goluses, Nicholas, 37
Gonzales, Jerry, 215
Göteborg Conservatory, 139-41
GöteborgsMusiken Chamber Ensemble, 139
Gothenburg College of Music, 18
Gothenburg Opera, 139
Gounod, Charles, 145
Graf, Erich, 101, 159
Graf, Peter-Lukas, 103
Grafenauer, Irena, 106-07
Grahek, Matej, 106
Granados, Marco, 108
Grant Park Symphony Orchestra, 25, 208, 210
Grauwels, Marc, 111
Greenberg, Susan, 113
Guildhall School of Music and Drama, 20, 61, 63, 198, 230

H)

Hague Royal Conservatory, The, 27
Haifa Chamber Orchestra, 211
Haitink, Bernard, 40
Hamburg Filarmonisches Staatorchester, 86
Hammerth, Johan, 17
Hammond, Jeffrey, 2
Hanson, Howard, 221
Harid Conservatory, 95
Hartt School, The, University of Hartford, Connecticut, 228
Hebert, William, 58-59, 125
Heifetz, Jascha, 94
Heim, Fred, 229
Hendrix, Jimi, 3, 70
Hindemith, Paul, 65, 176
Hochschule Academy of Music and Theater, Hamburg, 81
Hoeppner, Susan, 116
Hofer Symphoniker, Germany, 52
Holiday, Billie, 215
Hollywood Bowl Orchestra, 73, 113, 126
Honegger, Arthur, 141
Hotteterre, Jacques Martin, 89
Houston Ballet Orchestra, 171-72

Houston Symphony, 12, 75-77, 136 ; Houston Symphony Chamber Players, 75
Hudson Valley Philharmonic, 152
Huntington Symphony Orchestra, West Virginia, 130

I)

I Solisti Italiani, 181
Ibert, Jacques, 144
Illinois, Urbana-Champaign, University of, 154
Indianapolis Symphony Orchestra, 166
Interlochen National Music Camp, 154, 221
Iowa, University of, 70
Israel Philharmonic Orchestra, 4
Israel Sinfonietta, 81

J)

Jerusalem Academy of Music, 4
Jethro Tull, 1-3, 127
Johnnie Otis Show, The, 184
Johnson, Bruce, 184
Jones, Quincy, 135
Juilliard School, The, 10, 30-31, 50-51, 93-94, 98, 101, 116, 118, 120, 131, 136, 159, 161-62, 167, 168-69, 185, 226

K)

Kane, Trudy, 118
Kansas City Philharmonic, 23, 164, 183
Karajan, Herbert von, 163
Kaufman, Mindy, 120
Keilberth, Joseph, 104
Kemler, Katherine, 122
Kennesaw State University, 193
Khaner, Jeffrey, 124
Kincaid, William, 10-11, 56, 97, 104, 136, 224
King Chubby, 72

Kirk, Roland, 2
Klemm, Conrad, 235
Klemperer, Otto, 104
Kooiman. Ton, 83
Krall, Diana, 120
Krell, John, 192
Krieger, Norman, 190
Kuhlau, Friedrich, 56
Kujala, Stephen, 126
Kujala, Walfrid, 129

L)

Lancie, John de, 59
Langevin, Robert, 35, 131
Lanier, Jaron 72
Larson, Rhonda, 133
Laurent, Georges, 222
Lavaillotte, Lucien, 21
Laws, Hubert, 135
Lenehan, John, 39
Ligeti, György, 63
Lille Orchestra, 89
Ljublijana Academy of Music, Slovenia, 106
Lloyd Webber, Andrew, 84
Lolya, Andy, 53
London Debussy Trio, 143
London, Instrumental Quintet of, 143
London Philharmonic Orchestra, 44-45, 197
London Sinfonia, City of, 4
London Sonata Group, 143
London Symphony Orchestra, 60-62, 139, 154; LSO Discovery, 60
London Winds, 63
Longy School of Music, Boston, 221
Lora, Arthur, 161-62
Los Angeles Chamber Orchestra, 113, 183

Los Angeles Opera, 113
Los Angeles Philharmonic, 73-74, 113-14, 168, 170, 232-33
Los Angeles, University of California (UCLA), 114, 184, 206-7
Lot, Louis, 22
Louisiana State University, 122
Lyric Opera, Chicago, 25

M)

Madison Symphony, Wisconsin, 55
Madonna, 120
Mages, Sam, 127-28
Mahler, Gustav, 77, 100, 141, 165, 189, 229
Malmö Conservatory, 139
Manhattan School of Music, The, 29, 53, 131, 149-51, 161, 188
Mann, Herbie, 137, 214
Mannes College of Music, 95
Marcusson, Göran, 139
Mariano, Joseph, 37-38
Marten, Frank, 107
Martha's Vineyard Festival, 113
Masur, Kurt, 45, 189
Mayer, John, 40
McCartney, Paul, 78, 80
McKee, Robin, 142
McKeesport Symphony, 99
Mehta, Zubin, 114
Memphis Symphony Orchestra, 171, 201
Mendelssohn, Felix, 26
Metropolitan Opera Orchestra, 118-19, 161, 217
Michalak, Thomas, 51
Michigan, University of, 12, 211-12
Midsummer's Music Festival, 25
Milan, Susan, 143
Miller, Mitchell, 10-11

Mills College, 174
Mills, Roger, 127
Milwaukee Symphony Orchestra, 120, 183
Minnesota Orchestra, 65
Mitropoulis, Dmitri, 229
Molloy, Matt, 146
Monroe, Ervin, 149
Mons Royal Conservatory, 111
Monteux, Claude, 152, 228-29
Monteux, Pierre, 153, 174-75; Pierre Monteux School, 152
Montreal Conservatory, 132
Montreal Symphony, 35, 58, 131
Morris, Bob, 229
Mostly Mozart Festival Orchestra, 97, 124, 183
Moyse, Marcel, 61, 143-45, 201, 231
Mozart, Wolfgang Amadeus, 63, 75, 88, 104, 107, 118, 157-58, 162-63, 165, 191, 196, 239
Mozarteum, Salzburg, 106
Mozarteum Orchestra, 149
Munich Philharmonic Orchestra, 156
Murchie, Robert, 154
Murray, Alexander, 154
Music Academy of the West, Santa Barbara, 73, 179
Music Hochschule, 20
Musicians from Marlboro, 95

N)

Nash Ensemble, 63
National Academy of Arts & Sciences, 206
National Arts Centre Orchestra, 186
National Endowment for the Arts, 130
National Flute Association, 23, 29, 37, 218; Lifetime Achievement Awards, 10, 20,

index

23, 29, 55, 68, 99, 129, 164, 221; Newly Published Music Competition, 161; Young Artists Competition, 168, 179, 199, 211-12

National Symphony, 179

National Youth Orchestra, U.K., 84

NBC Symphony, 161, 174-75, 229

Nelson, Sandy, 185

Netherlands Radio Philharmonic Orchestra, 86

New England Conservatory of Music, 152, 222, 236

New Jersey Symphony, 50-51, 101

New Orleans Symphony Orchestra, 56, 183

New School, The, Manhattan, 108

New World Symphony, Miami, 168-69, 179

New York City Ballet, 29

New York City Opera, 113, 228

New York, High School of Music and Art, 167

New York Philharmonic, 10, 14, 29, 50-51, 93, 101, 118-19, 120, 131, 135, 181, 188, 201, 229

New York, State University, Stony Brook, 226

New York University, 29, 93

New York Virtuosi, 93; Virtuosi Quintet, 93

New Zealand Symphony Orchestra, 204

Newman, Alfred, 206

Newport Music Festival, 139

Nielsen, Carl, 60

Nobis, Ricklen, 101

Norrlands Opera, 18

North Carolina at Chapel Hill, University of, 218

North Carolina School of the Arts, 52, 223

Northern California Honor Orchestra, 113

Northwestern University, Chicago, 129

Nyfenger, Thomas, 53, 76, 159-60

O)

Oakland Symphony, 114

Oberlin Conservatory, Ohio, 46, 68, 142, 221

Occidental College, 185

Ohio State University, 152

Ojai Festival, 113

Oklahoma All-State Orchestra, 142; All-State Band, 142

Orford International Summer Festival, 131

Ormandy, Eugene, 104

Orpheus Chamber Orchestra, 34, 159, 188

Oxford Flute Summer School, 122

Ozawa, Seiji, 35

P)

Pacific Symphony, 73

Paganini, Niccolò, 37, 70

Pahud, Emmanuel, 156

Palma-Nidel, Susan, 159

Panitz, Murray, 49, 58-59, 181-82

Paris, Academie de, 88

Paris Conservatoire Orchestra, 20, 46

Paris, Orchestra de, 43, 68

Paris, Orchestre de l'Opera, 42

Parloff, Michael, 161

Pasadena Symphony, California, 73

Paul Winter Consort, 133

Peck, Donald, 164

Peabody Conservatory of Music,

65, 95, 152, 190, 221
Pellerite, James, 166
Pennsylvania All-State Band, 166
Philadelphia, Chamber Symphony of, 149
Philadelphia Orchestra, 55-56, 58, 104, 124, 166, 181-82
Philadelphia Woodwind Quintet, 55
Philharmonia Orchestra, 197
Pittsburgh Symphony, 10, 58, 97, 99, 124, 131, 217, 222
Planxty, 148
Polish Radio National Symphony Orchestra, 166
Powell, Verne Q., 22
Price, Leontyne, 175
Prokofiev, Sergei, 140, 142, 152, 175
Puccini, Giacomo, 140
Puente, Tito, 214-15
Puerto Rico Symphony Orchestra, 166

Q)

Quantz, Johann Joachim, 89
Queens College, 93
Quintet of the Americas, 108

R)

Rampal, Jean-Pierre, 42, 46, 79, 94, 149, 224-25 ; International Flute Competition, 42
Ransom, Catherine, 168
Rasch, Alison Young, 171
Ravel, Maurice, 125
Ravinia Festival, 75
Reade, Paul, 63-64
Renzi, Paolo, 175
Renzi, Paul, 174
Rice University, 232
Rimsky-Korsakov, Nikolai, 140

Robison, Paula, 177
Rochester Philharmonic Orchestra, 120-21
Romeo, Peggy, 172
Root, Marten, 83
Roseman, Ronald, 54, 96
Roussel, Albert, 144
Rowe, Elizabeth, 179
Royal Academy of Music, Amsterdam, 27
Royal Academy of Music, London, 20, 49, 199
Royal Ballet Orchestra, 101, 149-50, 159
Royal College of Music, London, 44, 84, 143
Royal College of Music, Stockholm, 17
Royal Concertgebouw Orchestra, Amsterdam, 27
Royal Conservatory of Music, 186
Royal Dutch Conservatory, 154
Royal Northern College of Music, Manchester, 199, 230
Royal Opera, Stockholm, 17
Royal Opera House, Orchestra of the (Covent Garden), 39-41
Royal Philharmonic Orchestra, London, 143, 145, 197
Royal Philharmonic Orchestra, Stockholm, 17, 19, 141
Rütters, Matthias, 7

S)

Sabreen, 219
Sacramento, California State University, 236-37
Saint Lawrence Quartet, 95
Saint Louis Symphony Orchestra, 23, 183, 201-3, 221
Samuels, Dave, 214
San Antonio Symphony Orchestra, 53, 201
San Diego, California State

index

University, 152
San Francisco Ballet, 65
San Francisco Conservatory of Music, 65
San Francisco Opera, 65, 175
San Francisco Symphony, 65, 114, 142, 174-75, 193
San Francisco State University, 174
Sanderman, David, 154
Santa Fe Symphony, 52
Schocker, Gary, 181
Schubert, Franz, 14
Schuster, Savely, 23
Elisabeth Schwarzkopf, 37, 104
Seattle Symphony, 97, 164
Serkin, Rudolph, 95
Sharp, Maurice, 10-11, 48
Shenzhen Symphony, 211
Sheshbesh, 4-5
Shostac, David, 183
Shostakovich, 40, 76, 141, 175
Shreveport Symphony, 8
Shulman, Nora, 117, 186
Siebert, Renée, 14, 188
Sigismonti, Henry, 73
Sinatra, Frank, 62
Sinatra, Nancy, 184
Sinfonia Finlandia, 88
Singapore Symphony Orchestra, 211
Skala, Emily, 190
Slovenia, Big Band RTV, 106
Slovenian Philharmonic Orchestra, 106-7
Slovenian Radio Symphony Orchestra, 81
Smith, Christina, 193
Smith, Joshua, 195
Snowden, Jonathan, 197
Solisti New York Orchestra, 223
Solti, Georg, 74

South-German Chamber Orchestra, 4
Southern California, University of (Thornton School of Music), 73, 216, 232
Southworth, Clare, 199
Sparks, Mark, 201
Speculum Musicae, 159
Spoleto Festival Orchestra, Italy, 52, 177; U.S., 177
Stamford Symphony, 101
Stanford University, California, 29, 174
Stern, Isaac, 6-7
Still, Alexa, 204
Stockholm Conservatory, 139
Stokes, Sheridon, 206
Stolper, Mary, 208
Stratford-upon-Avon, International Flute Festival in, 78
Strauss, Richard, 142, 165
Stuttgart Ballet, 159
Symphony of the Air, The, 229
Syracuse University, 50

T)

Ta, Jin, 211
Takeishi, Satoshi, 72
Tanglewood Festival, 58, 114
Tchaikovsky, Piotr Ilyich, 13, 190-91
Teatro alla Scala, 86
Telemann, Georg Philipp, 89, 224-25, 236
Temple University, Philadelphia, 58
Texas Southern University, 136
Three Rivers Young People's Orchestra, Pittsburgh, 99
Tilson Thomas, Michael, 114, 169
Timm Wind Quintet, 122
Toledo Symphony, 171
Torno, Larry, 221

Toronto Symphony Orchestra, 117, 186
Toronto, University of, 116, 186
Toscanini, Arturo, 161, 174, 229
Triangulo, 108
Trinity College of Music, Greenwich, 32, 48
20th Century Fox Orchestra, 207
Tyner, McCoy, 214

U)

Umeå Sinfonietta, 18
Un Mundo, 108
Underwood, Keith, 53, 193-94
U.S. Capital Wind Orchestra, 211
Utah Symphony, 101, 159

V)

Vail Valley Music Festival, Colorado, 238
Valens, Ritchie, 184
Valentin, Dave, 214
Vassar College, 152
Venezuela, National Orchestra of, 108
Verdi, Giuseppe, 140, 175
Vermont Chamber Orchestra, 97
Villa-Lobos, Heitor, 23

W)

Wagner, Richard, 165
Wagner, Roger, 114
Walker, Jim, 216
Wayne State University, 12
West German Sinfonia, 181
Wetter-Smith, Brooks de, 218
Wiesbaden Academy of Music, 6
Wilkins, Frederick, 167
Williams, John, 73
Willoughby, Robert, 65-67, 142, 201, 221

Wills, Vera, 172
Wilson, Ransom, 53, 201, 223
Wincenc, Carol, 169, 226
Wingra Quintet, 55
Winters, Barbara, 74
Wion, John, 228
Wisconsin-Madison, University of, 55
Wummer, John, 229
Wye, Trevor, 141, 230

X)

Xiamen Symphony, 211

Y)

Young Musicians Foundation, 114

Z)

Zentner, Anne Diener, 232
Ziegler, Matthias, 234
Zucker, Laurel, 236
Zukerman, Eugenia, 238
Zukovsky, Michelle, 74
Zurich Conservatory, 234-35